Dyes & Paints

A Hands-On Guide to Coloring Fabric

Elin Noble

**FIBER
STUDIO
PRESS®**

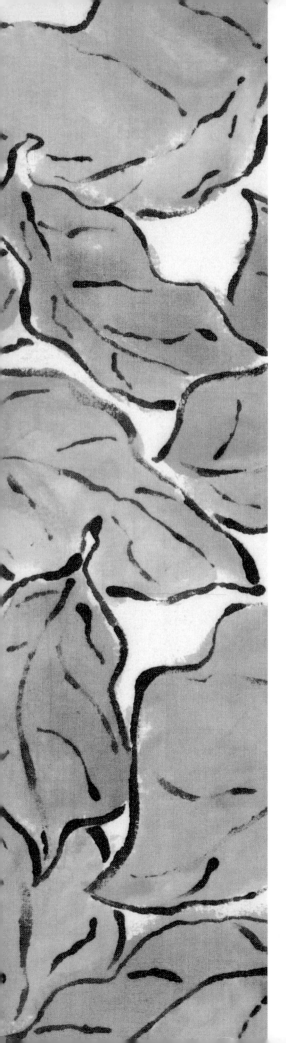

Credits

Editor-in-Chief .... Kerry I. Smith
Technical Editor .... Melissa A. Lowe
Managing Editor .... Judy Petry
Copy Editor .... Tina Cook
Proofreaders .... Leslie Phillips
    Melissa Riesland
    Kathleen Pike
Design Director.. Cheryl Stevenson
Text and Cover Designer .... David Chrisman
Design Assistant .... Keather Weideman
Illustrators .... Laurel Strand
    Robin Strobel
Photographer .... Brent Kane

Dyes & Paints: A Hands-On Guide
to Coloring Fabric
©1998 by Elin Noble
Martingale & Company, PO Box 118
Bothell, WA 98041-0118 USA
Printed in Hong Kong
03 02 01 00 99 98   6 5 4 3 2 1

**FIBER
STUDIO
PRESS®**

Library of Congress Cataloging-in-Publication Data
Noble, Elin
    Dyes & paints : a hands-on guide to coloring
fabric / Elin Noble.   p.   cm.
    Includes bibliographical references and index.
    ISBN 1-56477-103-2
    1. Dyes and dyeing—Textile fibers.   2. Dyes
and dyeing—Cellulose.   3. Dyes and dyeing,
Domestic.   4. Textile painting.   I. Title.   II. Title:
Dyes and paints.
TT853.N63   1997
746.6–DC21   97-27637
                    CIP

MISSION STATEMENT

WE ARE DEDICATED TO PROVIDING
QUALITY PRODUCTS AND SERVICE BY
WORKING TOGETHER TO INSPIRE
CREATIVITY AND TO ENRICH THE
LIVES WE TOUCH.

Dedication

This book is dedicated to the memory of my chosen sister, Barbara.

Acknowledgments

The basis for the directions in this book were originally written by Don Wiener, one of the founders of PRO Chemical & Dye, Inc. (PRO Chem). Over the years, I have always turned to Don for assistance with my personal dyeing experiments and business. So, when I was invited, in 1991, to manage the dye laboratory at PRO Chem and work with Don, I was elated. Don, who had been my mentor and friend for years, was now a daily source of inspiration and enlightenment. He is an important part of this book. The knowledge and experience Don has shared with me, and what I gained from working at PRO Chem, I now share with you.

This book marks an emotional and eventful crossroads in my life. Its publication is the result of the unequivocal support and love of many people: some helped in technical ways, others provided wise counsel or quiet space. Many thanks to my family for their help and wisdom, from the long conversations with my mother, Maurine Noble, to the personal and professional support from my husband, Ron—it has always sustained me. My sincere gratitude to Adelle and Don Wiener, Steve Grunebach, Debi Hogan, Karen Perrine, Vicki Jensen, and Nancy Rodrigues. I thank the late Barbara Eckhardt for her friendship, support, contagious enthusiasm, and—most of all—for sharing her courageous spirit.

A very special thanks to the staff at PRO Chemical & Dye, Inc., whose tireless efforts in helping me track down information and re-check numbers and facts, made this book a reality.

I am fortunate to have textile-artist friends who continue to inspire me with their work and inventiveness; I am indebted to those artists whose exceptional work helps illustrate this book.

My appreciation goes to Melissa Lowe, whose excitement about *Dyes & Paints*, faithfulness to the manuscript, lighthearted approach to editing, and patience during my recovery made working with Fiber Studio Press a pleasure.

Finally, thank you to my students, who asked many questions and also helped answer them. I am grateful to all of you who, like me, get excited over a length of a beautifully dyed cloth.

Contents

▲ *Aqua Detritus*
by Karen Perrine, 1996, Tacoma, Washington,
34" x 171". **Method**. Fiber-reactive dye on cotton.
Machine pieced, hand appliquéd, and machine
quilted. Photo by the artist.

> *Detail of Aqua Detritus*

Foreword

"Surface design" is a relatively new term for an activity as old as man, the coloring and embellishing of surfaces that are a functional part of daily life. Although technically the definition encompasses any coloring applied to paper, basketry, leather, or even metals, most surface designers today work with fabric. Fiber is familiar, closer to us than any other medium, and color is what we see first. No wonder that coloring fabric has a magical appeal.

Any contemporary gathering of surface designers will include a number of artists, usually women, who discovered dye twenty to thirty years ago during the tie-dye craze of the 1960s and early 1970s. Elin Noble and I are charter members of the club. However we came to get our hands immersed in it, dye has held us captive ever since. We share stories of lengthy searches for cotton fabrics in an era of polyester and remember heroic quests for written instructions. Dyes of dubious provenance and mysterious content were widely available then, but accurate information on what, why, and how was nonexistent. As the tie-dye fad faded, supplies became hard to find and sources disappeared overnight. We often had to begin all over again with a new type of dye, purchased by mail from a post office box in a small town hundreds of miles away. All of us from that era did lots of experimenting out of necessity.

Elin Noble began her colorful journey by accident, discovering dyes in the textile design program at the University of Washington. She was, and is, intensely curious, and dye quickly became her intellectual focus and passion. It became subject to The Elin Method: research extensively, ask lots of questions, read everything available on the subject, experiment exhaustively, keep good records, and teach. Her long friendship and working relationship with Don Wiener, a founder of PRO Chemical & Dye, Inc., has led to invaluable insights into achieving the most permanent, repeatable results, using ingredients efficiently and reducing variables.

To those who are new to dye and to those who are experienced, this book offers the gift of proven methods that speed us to the business of painting glorious cloth. Elin says this book arose from her students' questions. We thank her for her lovingly crafted answers.

Karen Perrine

Preface

I never meant to write a book. My schedule was full with managing the lab at PRO Chemical & Dye, traveling, teaching, and dyeing fabric. But my students kept asking questions (often, in fact, the same questions). This book is the result. It was born of and grew in response to your questions and encouragement.

Many of you, knowing I was working on a book in 1994, wondered what had happened when that book didn't appear. In 1995, several weeks before I was scheduled to work on the photo shoot, I became severely ill with Lyme disease. Initially, doctors could not find the cause of this sudden onset of varied and recurring symptoms. Not knowing what is wrong with you is really quite silencing.

But, thanks to a handful of dedicated people, the crisis passed. My health is slowly returning, which leads me here, to finishing this book (and, of course, the photo shoot). I vividly recall Karen Perrine's enthusiastic and soothing voice when we first discussed my need for help with the photo shoot. She gracefully and willingly offered her artistry, technical proficiency, and inquisitive, "itchy" mind. Karen's enthusiasm and support are important additions to *Dyes & Paints*.

Elin Noble

Introduction

Helpful Hint

Learning the Language

To help those readers who are not familiar with the terms that are common in the dye industry, I've included a glossary at the end of this book. See Appendix A, "Helpful Terms," on pages 151–53 for definitions of highlighted words.

Dyeing and coloring fabric is exciting, captivating, and extremely rewarding. *Dyes & Paints* focuses on the fundamentals of dyeing and coloring 100% **cellulose** fabrics with **fiber-reactive dyes** and **textile paints**. The techniques in this book can be used for coloring cloth or adapted for thread, yarn, ribbon, handmade paper, basket reed, and even wood.

Many people try dye and textile paint because the fabric colors or patterns they want are hard to find. When you are able to color and pattern your own cloth, you are no longer limited to what is in stock at the fabric store. Instead, you can produce fabric of any **hue value**, and **intensity** you desire.

Don't jump into these recipes expecting to reproduce a specific piece or style of hand-dyed or -painted fabric. Textile artists spend years cultivating and developing their technical ability and style. If you find a piece of hand-dyed fabric you love, buy and appreciate it! I continually find lengths of fabric from all over the world that are enriching and exciting. The color, pattern, and drape of these coveted fabrics are wonderful sources of inspiration.

This book guides you through a variety of dye and pigment applications. My aim is to give you a solid foundation for further exploration, especially the information you need for problem solving. There are some processes and technical aspects of coloring fabric that are beyond the scope of this book. For information on other types of dyes, application methods, and dyeing techniques, I encourage you to read the books listed on page 159.

I offer this book as a beginning, rather than as a means to an end. The techniques will give you a foundation, a jumping-off point, for developing your own style of dyeing and coloring fabric. I urge you to experiment and to build on these techniques. I hope that, as you gain experience, the technical processes become second nature, so you can focus on the soul of your work.

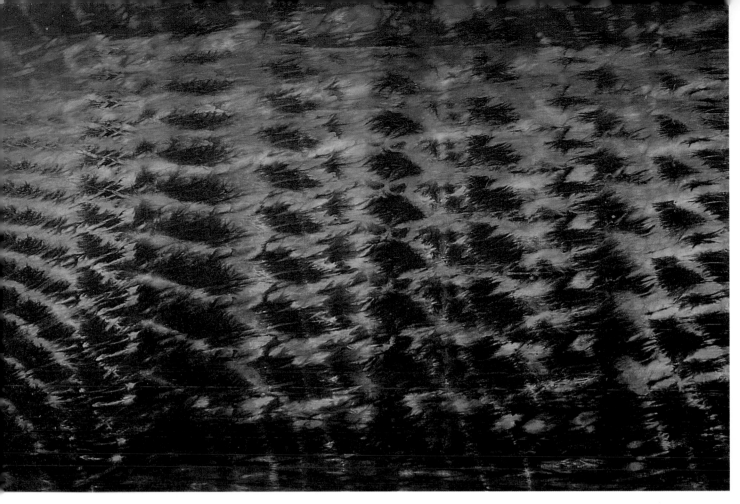

▲ Untitled yardage
by Michael Mrowka for Lunn Fabrics, 1994, Lancaster, Ohio. **Method**: Fabric bound, then dyed in multiple immersion dye baths. Photo by John Bonath at Mad Dog Studio.

◀ Untitled yardage
by Michael Mrowka for Lunn Fabrics, 1994, Lancaster, Ohio. **Method**: Fabric folded and clamped, then dyed in an immersion dye bath. Photo by John Bonath at Mad Dog Studio.

▼ Untitled yardage
by Stacy Michell for Shades, 1994, Marietta, Georgia. **Method**: Fabric dyed with direct-application technique. Photo by the artist.

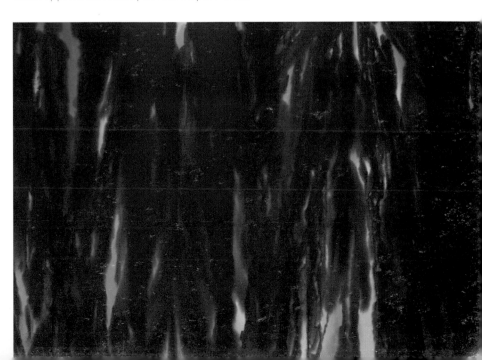

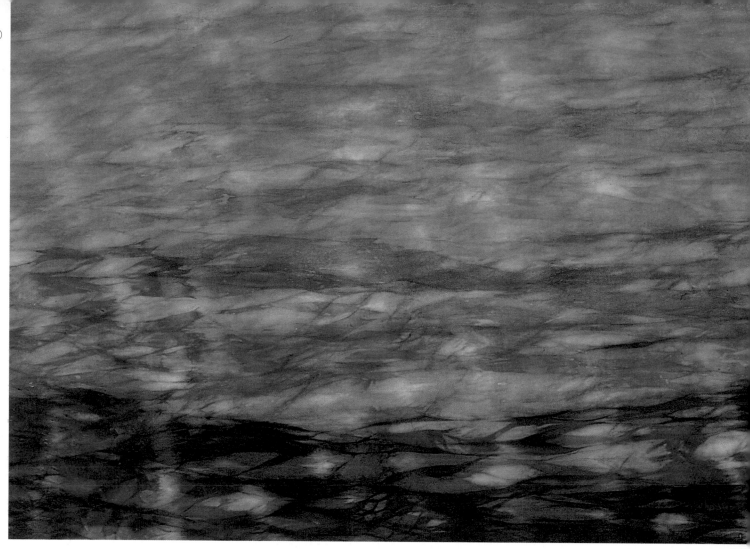

△ **Untitled yardage**
by Michael Mrowka for Lunn Fabrics, 1994, Lancaster, Ohio. **Method**: Fabric dyed in multiple immersion dye baths. Photo by John Bonath at Mad Dog Studio.

❯ **Untitled yardage**
by Stacy Michell for Shades, 1994, Marietta, Georgia. **Method**: Fabric dyed with direct-application technique. Photo by the artist.

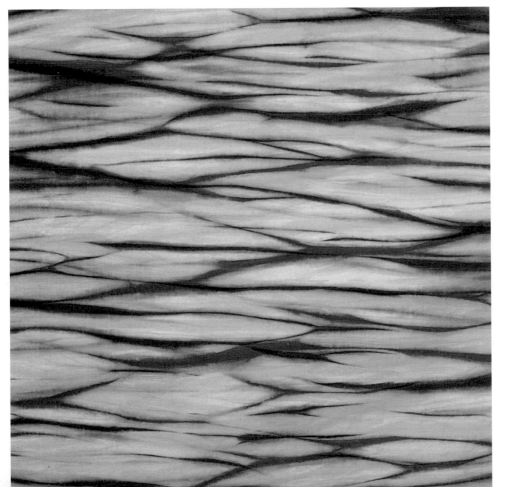

⋀ Untitled yardage
by Stacy Michell for Shades,
1994, Marietta, Georgia.
Method: Fabric dyed with direct-
application technique. Photo by
the artist.

⟨ Untitled yardage
by Michael Mrowka for Lunn
Fabrics, 1994, Lancaster, Ohio.
Method: Fabric bound on a pole,
then dyed in multiple immersion
dye baths. Photo by John Bonath
at Mad Dog Studio.

> *City Light*
by Carol Keller, 1996, Somerville,
Massachusetts, 68" x 58". **Method**:
Fiber-reactive dye on cotton muslin
and cotton sateen. Machine pieced
and quilted. Photo by David Caras.

⌄ *Encore*
by Janet Steadman, 1995, Clinton,
Washington, 64" x 45". **Method**:
Hand-dyed cottons by Liz Axford
and Connie Scheele. Machine
pieced and quilted by the artist.
Photo by Roger Schreiber.

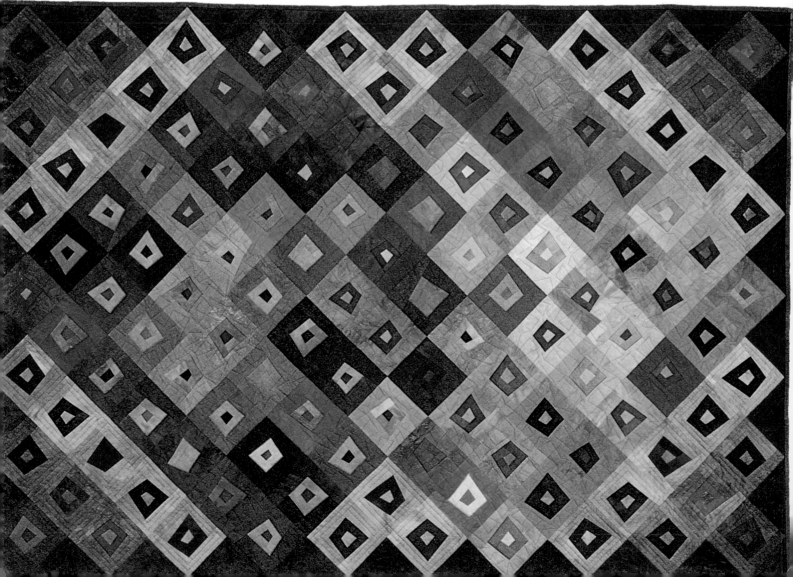

⌃ Within/Without 5
by Liz Axford, 1995, Houston, Texas, 25" x 25". **Method**: Fiber-reactive dye on cotton. Machine pieced and quilted. Photo by Hester and Hardaway.

⌃ Linear Study #7
by Nancy Crow, 1996, Baltimore, Ohio, 39" x 42". **Method**: fiber-reactive dye on cotton. Machine pieced. Hand quilted by Marla Hattabaugh. Photo by J. Kevin Fitzsimons.

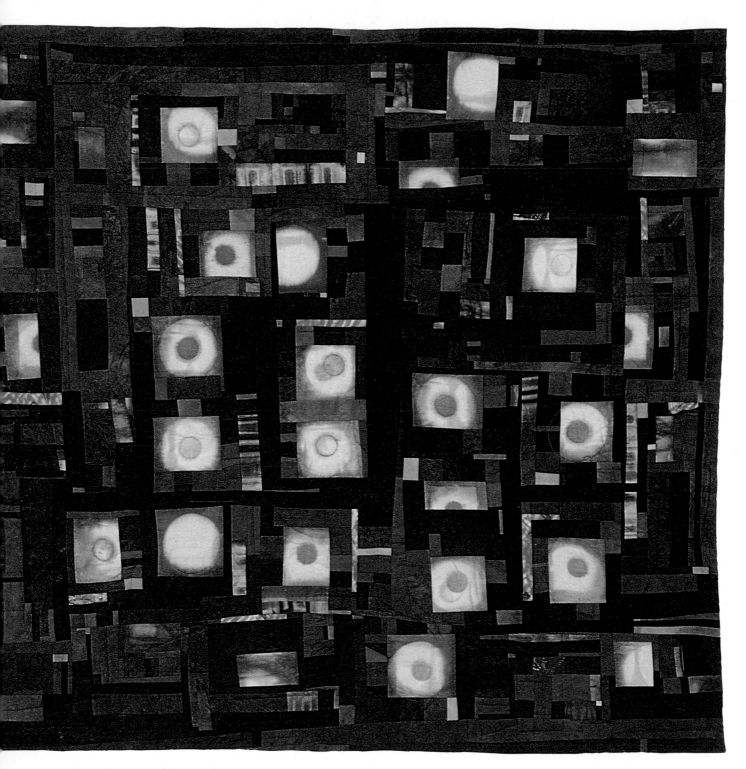

∧ Spheres and Atmospheres
by Rosemary Hoffenberg, 1995, Wrentham, Massachusetts,
61" x 58". **Method**: Fiber-reactive dye on cotton. Photo by
David Caras.

Part I: Basics

Using This Book

This book is organized into three parts: learning about dyes and paints (Part I), using fiber-reactive dyes (Part II), and using textile paints (Part III).

There are two basic methods of applying dyes to fabric: immersion dye bath (also known as vat or exhaust dyeing) and direct application (by hand). This book covers many techniques for and variations of both application methods, in addition to the standard dye bath: value gradation, hue gradation, immersion dyeing with a resist, tie dyeing, fold-and-dip dyeing, hand painting a design, color wash, monoprinting, stenciling, stamping, hand painting with a resist, and stamping with a resist.

Textile paints are usually applied by hand. As with dyes, this book covers many different techniques and variations, including stamping with leaves and shells, stenciling, sun printing, and marbling.

If you are new to coloring fabric, I urge you to read through the book rather than skipping directly to a specific application procedure, which I call "recipes." I know it's tempting to jump ahead, but there is helpful information on every page! Be sure to read "Protecting Yourself and Your Environment" on pages 16–17.

Understanding Dyes and Paints

Fiber-reactive dyes and textile paints color fabric in different ways. This does not mean that one is better than the other—each has advantages and disadvantages, depending on the desired result.

When you apply fiber-reactive dyes to fabric, a chemical reaction occurs and the dye molecules bond with the fabric molecules. The chemical bond cannot be broken or reversed, so the fabric is washfast. To remove color, as in a discharge process, you must destroy the color part of the dye molecule.

No creative artist can be anything so long as his hands have no share in shaping things.

Goethe

Helpful Hint

Substituting Dyes and Paints in the Recipes

As you work through the recipes, you may want to try stenciling with dye instead of with textile paint or immersing fabric in paint instead of in dye. Go ahead! The key is to match the viscosity of the dye paste or textile paint to the viscosity in the recipe, then set the dye or paint as needed. For example, mix a thick dye paste—the same consistency as textile paint—to stencil dye. Apply the dye paste as you would the paint, then **cure** the dye following the instructions for using thick dye paste. (Remember to wear gloves when using dye paste.) Or try dipping fabric in a bucket of diluted textile paint. Don't be frightened. Improvise, experiment, and enjoy yourself.

Safety equipment for working with fiber-reactive dyes

This type of chemical reaction does not occur with textile paints. Instead, textile paints contain a "binder" or adhesive that attaches insoluble particles of color to the fabric surface. This is an important difference. Textile paints leave an adhesive residue that may make fabric feel slightly to significantly stiffer; this is referred to as changing the **hand** of the fabric. Dyes do not change the hand of fabric.

Dye molecules are soluble in water (hydrophilic) and form transparent solutions. Textile paints are made of insoluble particles (hydrophobic) and are dispersed in water. While textile paints do not penetrate the fiber, they are available in intense colors—transparent and opaque—and are very easy to apply. The durability of the paint depends on the binder. As a rule, textile paints are more lightfast than dyes, but they have a tendency to "crock" or rub off in the wash.

To help you visualize the difference between dyed and painted fabric, I suggest thinking of the difference between a beet and a radish. Fiber-reactive dyes color fabric all through, like a beet. Slice a beet in half and it is the same color throughout. Textile paints color fabric like a radish—color on the outside fiber, and white, or undyed, fiber on the inside.

Protecting Yourself and Your Environment

If used properly, the fiber-reactive dyes, textile paints, and **auxiliary products** described in this book present a low risk to your health and to the environment. The dyes themselves are among the safest made; they are nonflammable and nontoxic. There is no need to be afraid of working with fiber-reactive dyes or auxiliary products. Water-based textile paints are even safer to work with than dyes—just don't eat them. (Textile paints do, however, have an odor that some people dislike. If this is a problem for you, work in a well-ventilated area.)

Because no chemical is entirely hazard-free, respect fiber-reactive dye and auxiliary powders, and treat them as chemicals, as you should household cleaning products. Use the following common-sense safeguards:

- Just as some people are allergic to pollen, chocolate, or nuts, some people are hypersensitive or have allergic reactions to dye and auxiliary powders. Avoid unnecessary exposure. Wear a dust/mist mask or respirator (see "Equipment" on pages 34–36) while working with these powders.
- Wear rubber gloves, old clothes or protective clothing, and even old shoes.
- Do not eat, smoke, or drink in an area where dyes and auxiliary products are used.
- Protect your work area with plastic sheeting.

- Do not use food utensils as dyeing equipment if you intend to return them to your kitchen. If you do use utensils from your kitchen, consider them donated to your dyeing. (I use this as an excuse to buy new kitchen gadgets and tools.)
- Wipe up any spills immediately. Liquid dye dries to powder that can be accidentally inhaled or ingested.
- Store dyes and auxiliary products in a cool, dry place, away from food and out of the reach of children or animals.
- Clearly label all solutions and containers of powder. *Do not* remove the supplier's name or hazard-warning labels.

When you have finished a dyeing procedure, you will have colored water left over; this is the exhausted dye bath. The color that is left is not harmful and is safe to discard down the drain into any septic or city disposal system. If you work outside, carry the dye bath into the house to discard it.

All suppliers have Material Safety Data Sheets (MSDS), which are available on request. This information sheet details precautions, potential health hazards, and clean-up information for *industrial* applications. The potential health and environmental hazards of wastewater from most home usage is considered insignificant.

RECOGNIZING AN ALLERGIC REACTION

An allergic reaction to dye is quite rare and is usually not severe. People experiencing an allergic reaction are usually responding to one of the auxiliary products, such as the activator, rather than the dye. Signs of sensitivity include coughing, a feeling of tightness in the chest, wheezing, and contact rash. If you experience any of these symptoms, move away from the area to fresh air. If the symptoms persist, consult your physician.

If you work with young children, have severe allergies, or are pregnant or asthmatic, take extra precautions. If working with young children, mix all the solutions in advance. Make sure the children wear old clothes, old shoes, and rubber gloves. If you have severe allergies or are pregnant or asthmatic, have someone mix the dye and auxiliary powders for you. As an alternative, consider using textile paints to color fabric instead of dyes.

Setting Up Your Work Space

Our mood—including the way we feel about our work space—greatly influences how we work, from the colors we choose to how productive we are. In an ideal world, we would all have a room or space we could set up as a dye studio. But no matter where you work, make sure you feel comfortable, and make sure you have enough space for the amount of fabric you plan to dye.

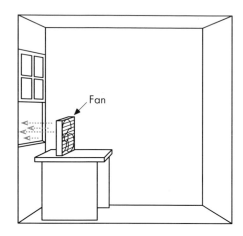

Fan

Getting Organized

It's a familiar cry, "I don't have enough room for this stuff!" There is no doubt that having to take things out and put them away each time makes starting more difficult. I have a rolling cart that I keep a couple of plastic tubs on; I can collect and roll out my supplies whenever I need them. Try not to squeeze your first attempt at these techniques into a few moments between other activities. If time is short, collect all the things you might need beforehand. When you are ready to start, time is not wasted looking for equipment.

It's best to work away from the primary living areas of your home—for example, in an unfinished basement, laundry room, or garage. You can work outside when the weather is nice. *Do not* work in a living area such as a kitchen, bathroom, family room, living room, or bedroom. This is a simple but important safety precaution (and it prevents accidental stains as well).

Proper ventilation is essential. Mix dyes in a well ventilated, but not windy, area. Create a local exhaust system by using a portable fan in a window. Place the fan so it pulls air from the room, away from you and out the window. Work facing the fan, so air currents are pulled away from your face.

Good lighting is essential. I like adjustable clamp lights; you can move them around so you never have to work in your own shadow.

Place a piece of homosote, foam core, or foam insulation board against one wall and use it for pinning up dyed fabrics.

It is convenient to have a water source, but it is not absolutely necessary. Improvise! You can use buckets and a garden hose with a nozzle.

If you do not have a work table, you can make one by placing a piece of plywood or a door on top of two sawhorses. A padded table with legs is ideal for direct-application techniques, though not essential. To make a padded surface, you need a piece of plywood—a 48" x 24" (122 cm x 61 cm) piece works well for half-yards of fabric—a piece of rug padding, thick felt, or ¼" (6 mm) -thick foam cut 2" to 3" (5 cm to 7.6 cm) larger than your plywood; a piece of muslin cut 6" to 7" (15 cm to 18 cm) larger than the padding; and a staple gun. Wrap the padding and muslin around the plywood and staple, pulling so both the padding and muslin are tight and even. If you don't have enough space to leave a padded work table set up, attach a strap to the back and move it as needed.

For an immersion dye bath technique, protect your table with a heavy plastic drop cloth and newspaper. For a direct-application technique, protect a padded table with plastic sheeting or a heavy plastic drop cloth. If you are pinning or taping fabric for wet techniques such as hand painting or monoprinting, cover the padded table with a heavy canvas drop cloth (rather than plastic). The canvas acts like a sponge, absorbing excess dye. Wash the canvas drop cloth after each use.

Cleaning Your Work Space

Since both dyes and textile paints are water based, you can clean with water. But be careful; dyes and paints tend to stain! Even the most pastel concentration can leave a trace of color on your clothes or work surface. You can usually remove dye and paint stains from your work surface with a bleach-type kitchen cleanser, but clothing stains are permanent. Remember Murphy's Law; if something spills, it's bound to end up where it's not wanted. Cover all your work surfaces and protect your clothes. Better yet, wear clothes you don't mind staining.

Understanding Color

Color is what dyeing and patterning fabric is all about. Because we associate certain colors with certain emotions, we tend to use those colors that make us feel most comfortable. This may be based on pleasant experiences or even on the inherent nature of warm (yellow, orange, red) or cool (blue, green, purple) colors. The challenge is to use colors you do not like. A funny thing usually happens—you end up liking or even falling in love with those colors you used to hate.

Traditional color theory helps us understand color relationships and why different color combinations are pleasing or disturbing. The following is a basic guide to color terms and relationships. For more information on color theory, see "Further Reading" on pages 159–60 and "Color Mixing Fiber-Reactive Dyes" on pages 41–45.

Analogous: Hues that are adjacent to each other on the color wheel. Yellow and orange are analogous colors. You can use analogous colors to produce harmonious color schemes.

Cool colors: A color that evokes cold. Blue and green are cool colors.

Direct complements: Hues that fall directly opposite each other on the color wheel. Blue and orange are direct complements. Direct complements mix to produce harmonious colors in the brown range. Try using a small amount of a direct complement to reduce the intensity of another color.

Hue: A synonym for color, hue is the pure state of a color.

Intensity: The saturation of a hue. The brightest colors are the pure hues on the color wheel. Less intense dye colors are less saturated and contain a small amount of their complementary color.

Monochromatic: Refers to a single color. A monochromatic color scheme consists of different values and intensities of one color.

Primary colors: There are three primary colors: red, yellow, and blue. All mixed colors fall within one of these color families.

Secondary color: A color that is a mixture of two primary hues. Orange, green, and purple are secondary colors.

Split complements: A hue plus two hues on either side of the primary hue's direct complement. Blue, yellow-orange, and red-orange make up a split complementary combination. Split complements often provide a subtler and more harmonious color scheme than a direct complementary scheme.

Tertiary color: A color that is a mixture of all three primary hues. Olive green, rust, and plum are tertiary colors.

Value: The lightness or darkness of a hue.

Warm color: A color that evokes heat. Yellow, orange, and red are warm colors.

> What tremendous variations from the smallest shading to the glowing symphony of colour. What perspectives in the dimension of meaning!
>
> Paul Klee

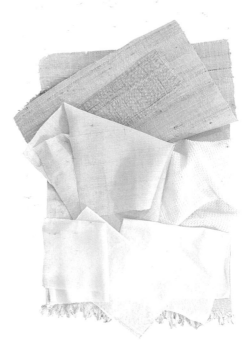

Different fabric weights
and weave structures

Choosing Fabric

This section provides an overview of the types of fabric that work best with fiber-reactive dyes and textile paints, and instructions on how to prepare these fabrics.

The recipes in this book are based on 100% cotton muslin, 45" (115 cm) wide, which is relatively inexpensive and available at most fabric stores. As you gain experience, try different fabric weights or weave structures. Experiment with jacquard, chintz, satin, velveteen, sheer, and embossed fabrics. The variations in weave may inspire designs or be appropriate for specific designs. Refer to "Calculating Measurements for an Immersion Dye Bath" on page 40. As a rule, the more tightly woven the fabric, the darker the color after dyeing.

FABRIC FOR FIBER-REACTIVE DYES

Fiber-reactive dyes are designed to work on 100% cellulose (vegetable) fibers, such as cotton, linen, viscose rayon, jute, ramie, or any combination of these fibers. These dyes also work well on silk, a protein fiber with cellulose **dye sites**. Many of the techniques I've described in this book can also be used or adapted for other protein fibers, such as wool, angora, mohair, and leather. The application procedures for these latter protein fibers are different than those covered in this book. For additional information, refer to "Further Reading" on pages 159–60 and consult a dye supplier.

Although fiber-reactive dyes do not work on synthetic fibers, they will work (to some degree) on polyester-cotton blends. After dyeing, these fabrics may have a uniformly heathery look or very irregular look depending on the consistency of the polyester-cotton blend. Also, synthetic blends will only dye a light value, regardless of how much dye is in the dye bath.

Stay away from fabrics treated with softeners and permanent-press, stain-resistant, flame-retardant, and water-repellent finishes. These finishes are difficult or impossible to remove and can cause tremendous headaches. My advice is to use another fabric. If you are determined to use a fabric with a permanent-press finish, follow the recipe on page 24.

Most fabric stores offer a selection of 100% cotton fabrics. Your local fabric store may have or may be willing to order fabric that has been specially prepared for dyeing—not treated with any of the finishes described above. Mail-order sources for prepared-for-dyeing (PFD) fabric are provided on page 158. Muslin is available as bleached (white) or unbleached (beige). The base color affects the final dyed color of a pastel shade. For example, use bleached muslin to dye a pastel tint such as sky blue. If you use unbleached muslin, the blue may have a greenish cast.

You may be able to purchase **mercerized cotton** fabric from your local fabric store. Mercerized cotton yields deeper colors and has improved strength and enhanced luster. It appears 25% darker than unmercerized cotton dyed with the same amount of dye. (Rayon also yields deeper colors.)

Different fibers have different chemical structures and react differently to heat and flame. These different reactions can help you determine the content of your fabric. Separate a couple of threads from your woven fabric. Twist them together so they form a tuft. Use tweezers to hold the tuft at the edge of a match. Note whether the fiber shrinks or melts, then place the tuft in the flame. Compare the characteristics of the flame, smoke, smell, and residue to the following table.

Mercerized versus unmercerized fabric. Mercerized fabric dyes 25% darker.

Determining Fabric Content

Fabric	Flame	Smell	Residue
Cellulose	Burns readily	Burnt paper	Soft gray ash
Protein	Burns only while held in flame, causes an irregular, spurting flame	Burnt hair	Black, crushable ash
Nylon	Does not burn easily, melts and drips	Strong sweet odor	Hard bead/drip shape
Polyester	Melts and burns with flame	Strong chemical odor	Hard bead
Acrylic	Melts and burns with flame	Strong chemical odor	Hard bead

FABRIC FOR TEXTILE PAINTS

Textile paints work on any fiber or combination of fibers, including cellulose, protein, and synthetics such as polyester, acrylic, and acetate. Avoid fabrics with permanent-press, stain-resistant, flame-retardant, or water-repellent finishes. As with dyeing, it is important to thoroughly clean the fabric before attempting to pattern it.

Overdyeing Commercial Fabric

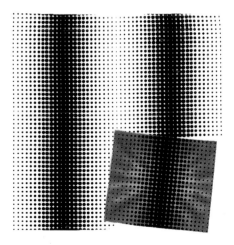

It is fun to experiment with **overdyeing** commercially printed and dyed fabrics. If you overdye different, incompatibly colored fabrics with the same color, you can end up with a harmonized palette.

Scouring Ribbon, Thread, and Yarn

You may want to dye ribbon, thread, and yarn for quilting or couching.

1. Wind the ribbon around a skein winder or piece of cardboard that is approximately 18" (45 cm) wide. Loosely knot the ends together.

2. Using synthetic or nylon twine, weave a loose figure eight (in and out and back again) through the ribbon. If the figure eights are too tight, you'll have tie-dyed ribbon! Knot the ends.

3. Tie the figure eights every 4" (10 cm) or so. Tying keeps the ribbon from tangling during scouring and dyeing.

4. Remove the skein winder or cardboard and scour the ribbon by hand. When you scour the ribbon, agitate by dunking the ribbon up and down or back and forth in the dye bath. If you agitate too much or stir in a circular motion, you'll have a tangled mess.

5. Remove the twine after the ribbon is dry.

Preparing Fabric

Scour your fabric to remove dirt, sizing agents, waxes, and oils before dyeing. Scouring may seem like an unnecessary step, but fabric that is not completely clean will not dye evenly. I recommend that you scour all fabric, even fabric prepared specifically for dyeing, before use. Scouring is an insurance policy worth investing in.

Do not use grocery store detergents for scouring fabric. These have added whiteners and brighteners that go on the fabric unevenly and may make dyeing uneven (especially for pastels). I particularly recommend avoiding powdered laundry detergents with little specks of color.

You can scour fabric by hand or machine. For small amounts of fabric, it's quicker and easier to scour by hand.

RECIPE FOR HAND SCOUR

Read through the directions and assemble all the necessary equipment and supplies before you begin.

Equipment

2-gallon (8-L) plastic bucket or enamel canning kettle
Clothesline and clothes pins (optional)
Dust/mist mask or respirator
Kitchen timer or watch
Long-handled spoon
Measuring cups and spoons or scale
Mixing box (see page 35)
Newspaper
Plastic drop cloth
Rubber gloves
Scissors
Spray bottle filled with water
Thermometer

Supplies

1 yard (91 cm) 100% cotton muslin
¼ teaspoon (1 g) PRO Dye Activator (see "activator" on page 37)
¼ teaspoon (1.25 ml) Synthrapol (see page 39)

Procedure

1. Cover your work table with the plastic drop cloth.
2. Set the mixing box on top of the drop cloth. Cut a small stack of newspapers to the inside dimensions of the box. Place the newspapers in the bottom of the mixing box and spray them with water. If you spill any of the powder during the mixing process, it will stick to the damp newspaper.
3. Measure 1 gallon (4 L) of 140° F (60° C) water into the plastic bucket. *Note:* If your water source is not hot enough, heat water on a stove or hot plate, then turn the heat off after the water reaches 140° F (60° C). Scour your fabric in the pot.
4. Wear a dust/mist mask or respirator and rubber gloves while working with the activator powder. Before opening the container, tap the lid so the powder settles to the bottom. Carefully open the container. Measure ¼ teaspoon (1.2 g) of activator powder into the bucket. Recap the container. Stir until the powder is dissolved.
5. Add ¼ teaspoon (1.25 ml) Synthrapol to the bucket. Stir.
6. Wearing rubber gloves, hand wash the fabric for about 10 minutes. Use the long-handled spoon to stir.
7. Rinse the fabric thoroughly in warm or cool water. It should feel squeaky clean.
8. You can use the fabric wet, or you can dry it and store for later use. To dry the fabric, hang it from a clothesline or use a dryer, following the manufacturer's instructions for the appropriate heat setting.

RECIPE FOR WASHING-MACHINE SCOUR

The following recipe is for the extra-large load setting on a washing machine. For smaller loads, see the chart on page 24. Contact your washing-machine manufacturer for your tub capacity (the number of gallons needed to fill the tub, not the total amount of gallons used for a wash load). Compare it to the chart and adjust the recipe if necessary.

Read through the directions and assemble all the necessary equipment and supplies before you begin.

Equipment

Clothesline and clothes pins (optional)

Dust/mist mask or respirator

Kitchen timer or watch

Measuring cups and spoons or scale

Rubber gloves

Scissors

Thermometer

Washing machine

Washing Machine Tub Capacity

To determine how many gallons or liters it takes to fill your washing machine, set it on small load with nothing in the tub. Let it fill. Measure, with a yard stick, the number of inches or centimeters and record the number. Set your machine on medium load and let it fill. Again, record the number. Continue this process until you have gone through all the size cycles. Allow your machine to cycle through the wash process (or do a load of laundry). Once the machine is empty, fill it one gallon (or liter) at a time from the sink. Count the number of gallons or liters until you reach the numbers recorded off the yard stick. Save this information!

Removing Permanent-Press Finishes

This recipe uses muriatic acid (hydrochloric 30%), a strong corrosive acid. **You must wear a respirator, rubber gloves, and safety glasses and use an exhaust fan while you work.**

1. Pour 2 gallons (8 L) of water into a large stainless steel or enamel pot. Carefully add 1 tablespoon (15 ml) of muriatic acid. To prevent splashing and possible explosion, **always add the acid to the water; never add the water to the acid.**

2. Place the pot on the stove, then submerge your fabric.

3. Heat the fabric to 185°F (85°C). Keep the temperature constant for 20 minutes, stirring the fabric occasionally.

4. Remove the pot from the heat and place it in a sink. Slowly add cold water, allowing the water to spill over and into the sink. Continue until the fabric is cool.

Supplies

10 to 15 yards (9.1 to 13.6 m) 100% cotton muslin for an extra-large load
2 tablespoons (18 g) PRO Dye activator (see "activator" on page 37)
2 tablespoons (30 ml) Synthrapol (see page 39)

Procedure

1. Cut the fabric into pieces, each 5 yards (4.5 m) or less.
2. Set the washing machine on the extra-large load, hot wash, and warm or cool rinse cycles. Check the water temperature after the machine fills. The water must be at least 140°F (60°C). You may need to heat water on the stove and add it to the machine.
3. While wearing a dust/mist mask or respirator and rubber gloves, add 2 tablespoons (18 g) of the activator powder and 2 tablespoons (30 ml) of Synthrapol. Let the machine agitate for 2 minutes.
4. Distribute the fabric evenly around the washing-machine tub.
5. When the machine has completed all the cycles, remove the fabric.
6. You can use the fabric wet, or you can dry it and store for later use. To dry the fabric, hang it or use a dryer, following the manufacturer's instructions for the appropriate heat setting.

Washing Machine Capacity Conversion Table

Machine Size	Water	Fabric
Small	12 gal (45.4 L)	9½ yd (8.7 m)
Medium	14 gal (53 L)	11 yd (10 m)
Large	17 gal (64.3 L)	13½ yd (12.3 m)
Extra-large	19 gal (72 L)	15 yd (13.7 m)

For each yard (91 cm) of fabric, use ¼ teaspoon (1 g) Activator and ¼ teaspoon (1.25 ml) Synthrapol.

WATER-DROP TEST

If you're not sure whether your fabric is completely clean, try this water-drop test. It can save you a lot of headache and heartache.

Using an eye dropper, place one drop of water on the dry fabric. Is it absorbed immediately, or does it sit on top of the fabric before it is absorbed? If it isn't absorbed immediately, there is a residue or finish on the fabric. Scour the fabric and test again before dyeing. Try using hotter water or a longer wash cycle, or try removing the finish as described at left.

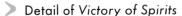

⌄ *Victory of Spirits*
by Debra Lunn, 1991, Lancaster, Ohio, 32" x 54". **Method:** Fiber-reactive dye on cotton. Machine pieced, hand quilted, and beaded. Photo by John Bonath at Mad Dog Studio.

❯ Detail of *Victory of Spirits*

< *Lobby*
by Heather Allen, 1992, Asheville, North Carolina, 76" x 90". **Method**: Fiber-reactive dye and textile paint on cotton. Machine pieced and quilted. Photo by John Lucas.

∨ **Make a Move**
by Angela Holland, 1992, Portland, Oregon, 24½" x 22¼". **Method**: Fiber-reactive dye on cotton. Machine pieced and hand quilted. Photo by David Bachhuber.

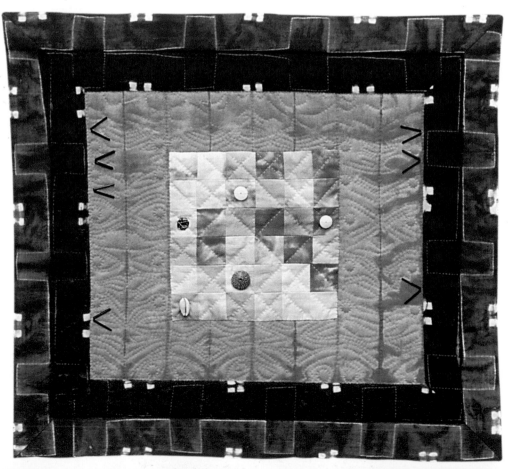

⋀ *On the Edge of Indecision*
by Debbie Photopoulos, 1992, Medford, Massachusetts, 60" x 28". **Method**: Fiber-reactive dye on cotton and silk. Hand appliquéd, embroidered, and quilted. Photo by the artist.

⋁ *A Summer's Day*
by Angela Holland, 1993, Portland, Oregon. **Method**: Fiber-reactive dye on cotton. Machine pieced. Photo by David Browne.

› *For Christiana Rossetti*
by Elizabeth Owen, 1991, Baton
Rouge, Louisiana, 33" x 29¼".
Method: Fiber-reactive dye on cotton.
Machine pieced and hand embroi-
dered and quilted. Photo by Ron E.
Dobbs.

⌄ *Beware of Falling Rocks*
by Connie Scheele, 1994, Houston,
Texas, 36" x 36". **Method**: Fiber-
reactive dye on cotton. Machine
pieced and quilted. Photo by the artist.

⋀ *Land, Sea and Sky*
by Linda Perry, 1995, Lexington, Massachusetts, 48" x 60". **Method**: Hand-dyed
and commercially dyed cottons, silk, and
rayon. Machine pieced and quilted, hand
appliquéd. Embellished with metallic leaf.
Photo by Joe Ofria at The Image Inn.

❯ *Pathways*
by Alison Goss, 1993, Cumming, Iowa,
52" x 52". **Method**: Fiber-reactive dye on
cotton. Machine pieced and quilted.
Photo by the artist.

⋀ *Views from the Hubble*
by Melody Johnson, 1994, Cary, Illinois,
60½" x 42¾". **Method**: Fiber-reactive
dye on cotton. Machine pieced and
quilted. Photo by the artist.

❯ *Dance Doctor*
by L. Carlene Raper, 1994, Putney,
Vermont, 55" x 75". **Method**: Fiber-
reactive dye on cotton. Machine pieced
and tied. Photo by Jim Thomas.

◄ *Pool II*
by Karen Perrine, 1996,
Tacoma, Washington,
31" x 50". **Method**:
Fiber-reactive dye and
textile paint on cotton.
Machine pieced,
hand appliquéd,
and machine quilted.
Photo by the artist.

> *David's House*
by Jan Myers-Newbury, 1994,
Pittsburgh, Pennsylvania, 49" x 57".
Method: Fiber-reactive dye on
cotton. Machine pieced and
quilted. Photo by Sam Newbury.

∨ *Seeing Is Believing*
by Jan Myers-Newbury, 1993,
Pittsburgh, Pennsylvania, 52" x 47".
Method: Fiber-reactive dye on
cotton. Machine pieced and
quilted. Photo by Sam Newbury.

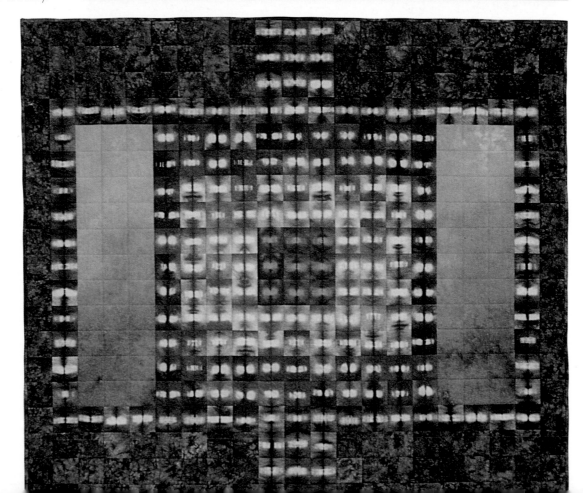

Part II: Dyes

In 1956, Imperial Chemical Industries Limited (ICI) discovered that a dye molecule containing certain chemical groups ("reactive groups") could react chemically with cellulose under alkaline conditions. The dye molecule reacts with the fiber molecule and becomes part of the fiber rather than remaining an independent substance trapped within it.

There are several types of dye available to home dyers. I recommend fiber-reactive dye, which is packaged under a variety of trade names. The most common brand is Procion. The instructions provided in this book are for Procion MX, also known as MX Fiber-Reactive Dye or cold-water dye.

MX Fiber-Reactive Dyes are applied at room temperature. There is no need to slave over a steaming dye bath or to chill your hands in cold water; the optimum dyeing temperature is between 70° and 105° F (21° and 40° C).

Fiber-reactive dyes are available in a wide range of colors. Other types of dyes available for home use may "bleed" or fade with repeated washing and exposure to light. Fiber-reactive dyes are highly concentrated and produce fabric that is resistant to bleeding and fading.

Dreams come true; without that possibility, nature would not incite us to have them.

John Updike

Working with Fiber-Reactive Dyes

There are two basic methods of applying dye to fabric: immersion dye bath and direct application. This book covers many different techniques for each method.

With the immersion dye bath method, fabric is placed in a dye bath containing water, dye concentrate, and auxiliary products for a specific amount of time. The fabric is then removed from the dye bath, rinsed, washed, and dried. The average dye-bath process takes approximately one hour.

With the direct-application method, a concentrated dye-stock solution is applied to the fabric. The dye-stock solution can be thick (like jelly), thin (like water), or any consistency in between, depending on the application technique. The fabric is left to cure for a specific amount of time. Excess dye is rinsed and washed out and the fabric is dried. Depending on the design and amount of fabric, this process takes from five minutes to several hours. Curing takes from four to twenty-four hours.

Equipment

The following is an overview of the equipment needed for working with immersion dye bath and direct-application techniques. A list of what is absolutely necessary is included at the beginning of each recipe. Don't be overwhelmed by the list. You can use many things you already have—old plates and saucers, sponges, pins, scissors, and newspapers—to test the dye techniques before investing in more expensive equipment. Necessity can lead to some interesting equipment and supplies!

It is surprising what useful objects and odd machines you can find in second-hand shops and yard sales. Look in industrial catalogs for strong plastic bins and troughs. Restaurant supply companies are a good source for buckets, spoons, and kitchen tools. Restaurant suppliers usually stock expensive and inexpensive large utensils. When you find interesting items or large items, pick them up. You will never be sorry.

Dust/mist mask: A paper mask is fine if you only dye fabric every once in a while. However, if you plan to do a lot of work with dye and auxiliary powders, I recommend that you purchase a Mine Safety and Health Administration (MSHA)/National Institute for Occupational Safety and Health (NIOSH) approved respirator with cartridges for dusts, mists, and fumes. These are available from suppliers that specialize in dye and safety equipment. Check your phone book for local suppliers or see "Resources" on page 158.

Dyeing Equipment

Dye buckets: Plastic, glass, or nonreactive metal containers (such as unchipped enamel or stainless steel) are preferable. Use a white bucket; the reflection of the dye color is truer. Plastic jelly buckets used in doughnut stores or joint-compound buckets used at construction sites work well. Avoid aluminum, tin, copper, and galvanized-metal containers. The dye will interact with the metal and produce duller colors. Have on hand a variety of one- to five-gallon (4- to 20-L) buckets. For **level dyeing**, there must be sufficient room in the bucket for the fabric to move freely. In addition, you must be able to stir the fabric without spilling the dye bath.

Fan: You need a large fan that you can position to pull the air away from your face as you work.

Measuring cups: Both plastic cups and Pyrex glassware are suitable. Some suppliers offer plastic safety beakers with markings. It is handy to have cup (250 ml) and quart (1 L) sizes.

I like to use 50-, 100-, and 250-milliliter graduated cylinders for more accurate measurements. Graduated cylinders are available in many sizes from dye- and scientific-equipment suppliers.

Measuring spoons: You need a set of plastic or stainless-steel measuring spoons.

Mixing box: Use a simple mixing box to limit airborne exposure to chemical powders. Cut off the top and one side of a 12" x 12" (30 cm x 30 cm) cardboard box, leaving a small "room" for mixing.

Newspapers: This is important for protecting your work space from stains.

Plastic drop cloth: Purchase plastic by the yard from a fabric store. This plastic does not have fold marks and will lie flat. If you purchase a heavy gauge (8 or 12 gauge and up), it will stay put without pinning. Use masking tape to secure your fabric to the plastic.

Record book: Keep a notebook with all the information you need to repeat a particular dye process. Over time, this book becomes a dyer's most essential piece of equipment! Write down the amount of fabric, dye, water, and different auxiliaries; the number of dye baths (if you are gradation dyeing); the length of time the fabric was in the bath; the curing time; the temperature (for direct-application techniques); and the date. Staple a swatch of undyed fabric and a swatch of dyed fabric next to the information.

Rubber gloves: You can use either disposable latex or reusable rubber gloves. Some suppliers carry reusable gloves that reach above the elbow. (I found shoulder-length gloves at a commercial fishing supply store.) These are great for large dye baths. Make sure the gloves fit well; they should feel like a second skin.

Scale: There are many different types of scales available (for example, kitchen, digital, counterbalance, and triple-beam). Choose a scale that you find easy to use. Make sure that it is accurate. A scale that measures from 1 gram to 2 pounds is handy. Use a bathroom

Keep a notebook detailing your dye processes.

Helpful Hint

Achieving Predictable, Repeatable Results

For predictable dyeing, you must control and repeat as many of the variables as possible. Variables include amount of dye, dyeing time, water, and air temperature, water source, and fabric. For instance, the temperature of cold water in Florida differs from that in Wisconsin, well water differs from a municipal water supply, and winter water differs from summer water. Also, our perception of cold varies from daytime to nighttime, from season to season, from Northeast to Southwest. This book includes specific time, water, and air temperature guidelines. If you follow these guidelines, you should have repeatable results. As you read this book, you may feel that I am repeating myself. You're right! Certain elements, if missed, can take the pleasure out of dyeing. Keep a notebook and record everything about your dye processes. Over time, this notebook will become your most important dyeing tool.

scale to weigh large amounts of fabric. (Weigh yourself while holding the dry fabric; then weigh yourself without the fabric. The difference is the weight of the fabric.)

Stirring tools: You need long-handled spoons (plastic, wood, and stainless steel), wooden dowels and/or chopsticks for stirring the dye bath, and small spoons, iced tea spoons, and swizzle sticks and/or wooden tongue depressors for stirring solutions. You may find that a wire whisk and a rubber scraper or spatula are helpful.

Thermometer: You can use any thermometer, as long as it measures temperatures from 60° to 185° F (16° to 85° C).

Timer: You need a kitchen timer, watch, or clock, preferably with a second hand.

Tools that are useful for specific techniques include: containers or jars of assorted sizes; paper cups or empty yogurt containers; rubber bands, bulldog clips, and pieces of wood; pushpins and/or masking tape; plastic plates or trays; an artists' stretcher frame or embroidery hoop; assorted synthetic artists' brushes and sponge brushes; assorted sizes of squeeze bottles and/or syringes; rubber or acrylic stamps; cellulose sponges; a plant mister or spray bottle; and rags, old towels, or paper towels.

A washing machine and dryer are handy, but you can use a bucket, clothesline, and plastic clothespins. Avoid wooden clothespins, which may absorb dye and stain your fabric. Always clean plastic clothespins before reusing them.

Supplies

I like to mark all dyes and auxiliary products with the date purchased. Each product has an optimum amount of time for use—the **shelf life**—based on its strength. Some products have much longer shelf lives than others. Be sure to store chemicals in properly labeled containers, and include any hazard information.

Dyeing Supplies

Activator: The activator (also referred to as the **fixative**) is a chemical that causes a molecular reaction to take place between fabric and dye. The activator is also used to scour fabric before dyeing.

You can use PRO Dye Activator or sodium carbonate (soda ash, washing soda, or sal soda). Do not use washing soda from the grocery store. It contains additives that would be detrimental to the results. I recommend using PRO Dye Activator because it is easy to dissolve.

Store the activator in a cool, dry place. Keep it in a container with a tightly fitting lid. You can use the activator as long as you can dissolve it. (Once wet, it will resemble concrete and will not dissolve fully.)

Baking soda (bicarbonate of soda): I use baking soda to make mixed alkali, which fixes dye to fabric. You can buy baking soda from the grocery store. Store it in a cool, dry place. I purchase a new box every year.

Citric acid or vinegar: If you work with silk, you can substitute citric acid or distilled white vinegar for the activator soak or mixed alkali powder in the direct-application dye recipes (see page 125). In general, citric acid is more stable than vinegar when mixed with dyes and produces better results. For more information on working with citric acid or vinegar, consult a dye supplier.

Fiber-reactive dye: The recipes in this book are written for Procion MX Fiber-Reactive Dyes. I prefer these dyes because they are versatile and easy to use, and they produce brilliant colors.

The major differences between brands of fiber-reactive dye are the application methods, temperatures of the dye bath, and the length of curing time. In addition to Procion MX, popular fiber-reactive dyes include Cibacron F (sold by PRO Chem as Sabracron F), Procion H (available in powder or liquid form), and Remazol. To adapt these recipes for use with Cibacron F dyes, modify the dye-bath temperature and curing time. The immersion dye bath temperature for Cibacron F is 105° to 120° F (40° to 50° C). Curing takes twenty-four to forty-eight hours and/or setting with a steam iron.

Most of the recipes in this book can also be adapted for use with Procion H dyes. The immersion dye bath temperature for Procion H is 170° to 180° F (77° to 82° C). The manufacturer recommends that the fabric be cured with steam. Consult your dye supplier for specific recipes and fixing procedures.

Remazol dyes work best with temperatures of 105° to 140° F (40° to 60° C). Consult a dye supplier for specific recipes and fixing procedures. Curing with steam is recommended, but I have been successful using stronger alkali and curing for 24 to 48 hours.

Store Procion MX dyes in a cool, dry place. Keep them in containers with tightly fitting lids. Under these conditions, the optimum shelf life of dye is two years. After two years, the color yield will begin to decline. The dye can still be used, but your results may not be repeatable.

Hand cleaner: The best approach is to wear gloves so you don't dye your hands in the first place! If you need to remove dye stains from your hands, purchase a specially formulated hand cleaner from dye suppliers. Do not use bleach to remove dye stains. If you make sure the container is closed between uses, the hand cleaner will remain at full strength for many years.

Metaphos: See "water softener." I recommend Metaphos (sodium hexametaphosphate) because it does not contain fragrances or other additives.

Presist: This liquid resist is a combination starch-paste (for creating bold patterns) and gutta (for creating fine-line patterns) resist. When applied to fabric and allowed to dry, Presist forms a barrier that inhibits dye penetration. Presist dissolves in the rinse without leaving a residue. Because it is amber, rather than clear, Presist is easy to see. This is my preferred resist for silk painting, beginning projects, and projects that involve children.

Store Presist in a cool, dry place. Keep it in a container with a tightly fitting lid, and do not allow it to freeze. According to the manufacturer, Presist has a one-year shelf life, but I have used two-year-old Presist with great results. Test a sample before using if your Presist is more than one year old.

Print paste: Made from urea, water softener, and sodium alginate (PRO Thick SH or F), print paste is used for direct-application techniques. You can make print paste from scratch (see pages 56–57), or you can buy a premeasured mix (PRO Print Paste Mix SH or F).

The SH products are recommended for cotton and the F products are recommended for silk. I have found the SH products to be the best all-purpose thickener; they work well on cotton and silk. For more information, consult a dye supplier.

Sabra Silk Resist: Frequently called a water-based, gutta resist, Sabra Silk is a colorless resist that works well for painting on silk or lightweight cotton. Like Presist, it forms a barrier on the fabric to create the pattern. Sabra Silk dissolves in rinse water without leaving a residue.

Store Sabra Silk in a cool, dry place. Keep it in a container with a tightly fitting lid, and do not allow it to freeze. According to the manufacturer, Sabra Silk has a one-year shelf life.

Salt (sodium chloride): Salt is an exhausting agent for the immersion dye bath recipes in this book. It has an electrostatic charge that pushes dye through the water and onto the fiber. Noniodized table salt is preferred but not absolutely necessary. (Iodine is a metal and can sometimes dull colors.) Noniodized table salt is available as kosher salt, canning or pickling salt, and "common" salt. Store salt in a cool, dry place. Keep it in a container with a tightly fitting lid. You can continue to use the salt as long as you are able to dissolve it.

Some dye manufacturers recommend Glaubers Salt (sodium sulfate) for increasing color yield, especially for turquoise dye. I don't feel that the minor color increase compensates for its expense and difficult dissolving characteristics.

Sodium alginate: This is a type of seaweed that thickens dye-stock solution for direct-application techniques. Sodium alginate is combined with urea and water softener to produce print paste. You can purchase sodium alginate as PRO Thick SH or F.

Store sodium alginate in a cool, dry place. Keep it in a container with a tightly fitting lid. If kept dry, sodium alginate will remain at full strength for many years.

Synthrapol: This is a special cleaning agent known as a "surfactant" (surface active agent). It is used in the scour recipe to prepare fabric for dyeing (see pages 22–24) and in the hot wash after dyeing to remove excess dye. You can also use Synthrapol in the dye bath to help ensure level dyeing.

Synthrapol has a very long shelf life. Over time, it may turn an amber color. You can continue using it even after it has changed color.

Urea: A synthetic nitrogen compound, urea ammonium carbamate is a humectant that prevents fabric from drying during the curing process. Urea also increases the solubility of the dye powder and is especially useful for mixing concentrated solutions of yellow, red, and black. In essence, urea makes the dye think it is in more water than it really is.

Store urea in a cool, dry place. Keep it in a container with a tightly fitting lid. Urea usually has a long shelf life. If you notice an ammonia-like odor after mixing, discard the solution and the urea.

Water: Your water source greatly effects your dye results. Municipal water sources add chlorine to kill harmful bacteria. The amount of chlorine can vary, producing lighter or darker results. MX fiber-reactive dyes perform best when applied and washed off in soft water. Impurities such as calcium, magnesium, iron, and copper take up space in the water, decreasing its ability to dissolve dye or auxiliary products. If you know you have hard water, purchase bottled or distilled water for mixing dye-stock solutions, or add water softener.

Water softener: If you live in an area with hard water, you need to add a water softener (Metaphos or Calgon) to the dye bath. I recommend Metaphos (sodium hexametaphosphate) because it does not contain fragrances or other additives. I also recommend using Metaphos in the print paste; it makes a smoother paste and improves your printing and painting results.

Store water softener in a cool, dry place. Keep it in a container with a tightly fitting lid. You can continue using the water softener as long as you are able to dissolve it.

Dyeing Brighter Colors

Some dyers add Ludigol (PRO Chem Flakes) to the dye-stock solution and paste mix in their direct-application dye recipes for brighter colors. Ludigol is a mild oxidizing agent that absorbs gasses from the air so dye molecules do not react prematurely and become "used up" before permanently fixing to the fabric. Ludigol is optional if you use MX Fiber Reactive Dyes, but it is necessary if you use Procion H Fiber-Reactive Dyes. Although the recipes in this book do not include Ludigol, you may want to use it if you live in a city with a great deal of air pollution. Add one teaspoon (2.5 g) per cup (250 ml) of prepared urea water or print paste.

Calculating Measurements for an Immersion Dye Bath

The immersion dye bath recipes in this book are based on industrial standards. These standards use the weight of the fabric to determine how much dye, auxiliary products, and water are needed to achieve a certain hue or value. This is referred to as "percent on weight of goods or fabric" (%OWG or %OWF). I translated the %OWG into teaspoons or grams and quarts or liters for home dyeing.

All the recipes are based on 45"-wide (115 cm) 100% cotton muslin. The weight of three yards (2.74 m) of 100% cotton muslin is approximately one pound (454 g). I divided one pound by three to determine the amounts of dye, auxiliary products, and water necessary to dye one yard (91 cm) of cotton muslin.

Because these recipes are based on an estimate of the fabric weight, you may get slightly different results, depending on the type and weight of your fabric. For example, the basic dye-bath recipe is not adequate for one yard (91 cm) of 100% cotton velveteen. Because cotton velveteen is heavier than muslin, you need more dye, auxiliary products, and water to produce the same hue. See the table to calculate the amount of dye, auxiliary products, and water needed for different weights of fabric.

Calculating an Immersion Dye Bath for Different Fabrics

For each pound (454 g)* of dry fabric:

Value	Light		Medium		Dark**	
	English	Metric	English	Metric	English	Metric
Water	2.5 gal	9.5 L	2.5 gal	9.5 L	2.5 gal	9.5 L
Salt	1¼ cups	363 g	1¾ cups	550 g	2½ cups	725 g
Metaphos (water softener)	1 tsp	7 g	1 tsp	7 g	1 tsp	7 g
MX Fiber-Reactive Dye	1 tsp	2.5 g	5 tsp	12.5 g	2½ Tbl	22.5 g
PRO Dye Activator	2½ Tbl	23 g	5 Tbl	45 g	7½ Tbl	68 g

* Determine the weight of your fabric using a kitchen or bathroom scale.
** For black, double the amount of dye powder and extend the dyeing time to 90 minutes after adding PRO Dye Activator.

Using Direct-Application Techniques

The direct-application recipes in this book are based on industrial standards. These standards use the strength of a stock solution to determine how much dye, auxiliary product, and water are needed to achieve a certain hue or value. This is referred to as a "percent solution." I translated the percent solution into teaspoons or grams and quarts or liters for home dyeing.

You can prepare more or less dye-stock solution according to the amount of fabric you want to dye. One cup (250 ml) of dye-stock solution colors one and one-half to two yards (1.37 to 1.82 m) of 45"-wide (115 cm) 100% cotton muslin. See "Dye-Stock Solution" on pages 50–51.

Color Mixing

Fiber-reactive dyes produce transparent color. The more dye powder you use, the darker the color. Conversely, the less dye powder you use, the lighter the color. To take advantage of the flexibility of transparent color, you must understand color mixing and the characteristics of each color. If you purchase and learn to blend the seven colors described in this section (your dye color palettes), you can enjoy a wide range of hues and values.

At present, there are fifteen colors of MX fiber-reactive dye manufactured as "self-shade" colors. The term "self-shade" indicates that these colors will dye, *by weight,* the same shade, value, and intensity every time. All other MX fiber-reactive dye colors are mixtures of these colors.

Color mixing is based on blending the self-shade and mixed dyes in different combinations and amounts. You can use a traditional color wheel to help understand the relationship between colors. Pure primaries (red, yellow, and blue) are not available as dye colors. Choose the closest dye colors based on whether you want earthy (rich, dark) or jewel (bright, saturated) colors.

Remember that white does not exist as a dye. It is assumed the fabric is white. As mentioned previously, if your fabric has a yellow, blue, or other tint, it will effect the color of the dyed fabric. This may not be important for medium to dark values, but it is very important for light values.

Helpful Hint

Ordering Dye Powders

The dye colors are referred to by the manufacturer's name and number, with the color name and number in parentheses. To order dye powders from PRO Chem, use the information in parentheses. Use the manufacturer's name and number to order dye powders from another supplier.

EARTHY PALETTE

For earthy colors, I recommend Procion Yellow MX-3R (Golden Yellow 104), Procion Red MX-5B (Mixing Red 305), and Procion Blue MX-2G 125 (Mixing Blue 402c) or Procion Blue MX-G (Intense Blue 406). These dye powders are usually less expensive than brighter dyes.

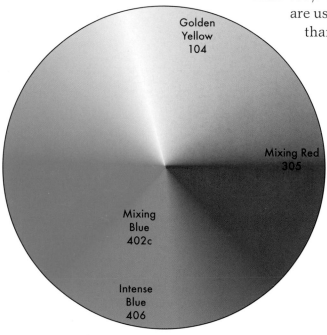

Earthy Palette Dyes

JEWEL PALETTE

For jewel colors, I recommend Procion Yellow MX-8G (Sun Yellow 108), Procion Red MX-8B (Fuchsia 308), Procion Blue MX-G (Intense Blue 406), and Procion Turquoise MX-G (Turquoise 410).

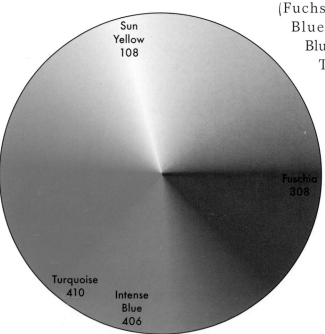

Jewel Palette Dyes

HELPFUL EXTRAS

You can always purchase more colors for easier mixing. For instance, it is difficult to mix a good brown and almost impossible to mix a good black. The first three dyes listed below are also manufactured as self-shade colors.

- Orange MX-2R (Strong Orange 202) is a brilliant orange with exceptional coloring power. A little goes a long way.
- Blue MX-R (Basic Blue 400) is a sky blue. This is not a strong dye and will not dye a dark value, but it is the only manufactured blue with a reddish cast.
- Brown MX-5BR (Reddish Brown 505) has a maroon cast and is good for a full spectrum of browns.
- Black MX-CWNA (Black 608) is a mixed color with a red cast. Black is by far the most difficult color to achieve with MX fiber-reactive dyes. This color is a full saturation of the right hues in proper proportion. If you use too much dye powder, the fabric takes on a reddish appearance, referred to as "bronzing." If you don't use enough dye powder, the fabric dyes gray rather than black.
- Mixing Gray 601, available from PRO Chem, is your neutral gray. No black, in MX fiber-reactive dye, dyes a neutral gray.
- Purple 804, Leaf Green 700N, and Chino 500, also available from PRO Chem, are convenient additions to a dye collection.

Helpful Hint

Characterizing Dye Colors

In dyeing parlance, to "characterize" a dye color means to determine the cast. Some manufactured dye colors, particularly reds, are difficult to characterize. If you are not sure whether a red is more yellow or blue, mix it with Mixing Blue 406. If the result is a grayed plum violet, then the red leans toward yellow. If the result is a bright violet, then the red leans toward blue.

Converting Decimal Amounts to Teaspoons

0.875 = ⅞ teaspoon
0.75 = ¾ teaspoon
0.625 = ⅝ teaspoon
0.5 = ½ teaspoon
0.375 = ⅜ teaspoon
0.25 = ¼ teaspoon
0.125 = ⅛ teaspoon

MIXING DYE COLORS

To control color mixing, you need to understand each dye's color, cast, and strength (ability to dye a dark value), as well as whether the color and cast are consistent from a pastel to a dark shade. The earthy palette is easier to mix because the dye powders—Golden Yellow 104, Mixing Red 305, and Mixing Blue 402c or Intense Blue 406—have higher solubility levels, similar reactivity rates, and lower substantivity than the dye powders in the jewel palette.

The first rule for mixing dyes is: *visual equilibrium is not necessarily physical equilibrium.* You need three times as much yellow as blue to produce a middle green. Varying the proportion of dye powder changes the color to a blue-green or a yellow-green.

The best way to learn color mixing is to experiment with different proportions. Turquoise 410 and Sun Yellow 108, bright hues in the jewel palette, have maximum absorption points, and will not dye dark shades no matter how much dye powder you use. Intense Blue 406 and Fuchsia 308, on the other hand, are highly concentrated dye powders that can easily overpower other colors (especially yellow). When mixing colors with Intense Blue 406, Fuchsia 308, and Mixing Red 305, use half the amount listed in the recipes until you are comfortable with the dyes' capabilities and ranges. When mixing colors with Sun Yellow 108, add very small amounts (drops) of a darker color(s) until the mixed color looks right to you.

The second rule for mixing dyes is: *avoid mixing more than three colors to produce one color.* It is always easier to repeat something with fewer variables. Also, the mixed color may dye unevenly. For example, if you want a brown dye, I recommend purchasing a manufactured color such as Brown 505, or mixing just two colors: Strong Orange 202 with Intense Blue 406.

The illustration on the facing page represents dye colors mixed from Sun Yellow 108, Fuchsia 308, and Intense Blue 406 (the jewel palette). The percentages in the accompanying chart indicate the amount of each dye used to create the numbered color.

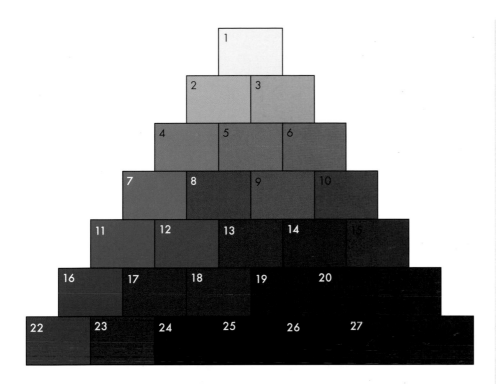

**Color Chart
Mixing Percentages**

Y = Sun Yellow 108
R = Fuchsia 308
B = Intense Blue 406

1	Y 100% R – B –		**15**	Y 60% R 40% B –	
2	Y 95% R – B 5%		**16**	Y 25% R – B 75%	
3	Y 98% R 2% B –		**17**	Y 20% R 20% B 60%	
4	Y 80% R – B 20%		**18**	Y 20% R 40% B 40%	
5	Y 85% R 8% B 7%		**19**	Y 20% R 55% B 25%	
6	Y 90% R 10% B –		**20**	Y 20% R 72% B 8%	
7	Y 70% R – B 30%		**21**	Y 20% R 80% B –	
8	Y 75% R 10% B 15%		**22**	Y – R – B 100%	
9	Y 80% R 15% B 5%		**23**	Y – R 20% B 80%	
10	Y 80% R 20% B –		**24**	Y – R 45% B 55%	
11	Y 50% R – B 50%		**25**	Y – R 60% B 40%	
12	Y 50% R 10% B 40%		**26**	Y – R 80% B 20%	
13	Y 50% R 25% B 25%		**27**	Y – R 95% B 5%	
14	Y 50% R 40% B 10%		**28**	Y – R 100% B –	

To determine the amount of dye powder you need to mix a numbered color:

1. Find the percentage mixing amount(s) in the chart at right.
2. Translate the percentage to a decimal by moving the decimal point 2 numbers to the left, for example, 40% = 0.4.
3. Multiply by the number of teaspoons or grams needed for a specific recipe.
4. For English measurements, convert the numbers to teaspoons using the chart on page 44. For metric measurements, use the numbers as is. The decimal numbers are equivalent to grams.

For example, color 12 is 50% Sun Yellow 108, 10% Fuchsia 308, and 40% Intense Blue 406. If you need 6 teaspoons (15 g), total, of dye powder for an immersion dye bath, you would multiply the color percentages by 6 for English measurements, then convert the decimal amounts to teaspoons.

English	Sun Yellow:	6 x 0.5 = 3 (3 tsp)
	Fuchsia:	6 x 0.1 = 0.6 (⁵⁄₈ tsp)
	Intense Blue:	6 x 0.4 = 2.4 (2³⁄₈ tsp)
Metric	Sun Yellow:	15 x 0.5 = 7.5 (7.5 g)
	Fuchsia:	15 x 0.1 = 1.5 (1.5 g)
	Intense Blue:	15 x 0.4 = 6 (6 g)

Mixing Basics

This section explains how to mix the basic concentrates, solutions, pastes, and mixtures used in immersion dye bath and direct-application recipes. All the fiber-reactive dye recipes in this book refer to this section; read it carefully before you begin working with dyes.

UNDERSTANDING THE VARIABLES

There are a number of variables that can affect your results when you work with fiber-reactive dyes. These variables include measuring techniques, air and water temperature, and reaction time (the reactivity rate) of the ingredients. One of the goals of this book is to provide simple, straightforward directions that help you control these variables—and avoid potential problems—as much as possible.

ACCURATE MEASURING

As you read through the recipes in this book, you will find both English and metric measurements. If you use the metric system and weigh the dye, auxiliary products, and fabric, you will have better control over the results, and it will be easier to repeat them. But do not feel as though you must work in metric. The English volume measurements provided here also work well, although your results may not always be exactly the same.

If you are dyeing fabric for a specific project, increase the recipe and dye more fabric to ensure you have enough from that dye lot. It can be very difficult to exactly match a previously dyed fabric.

Use level measurements for all the recipes in this book.

OPTIMUM WATER TEMPERATURE

Water temperature is one of the variables that can make it difficult to exactly reproduce a dye lot. As a general rule, the closer the temperature is to 105° F (40° C), the more efficient the chemical reaction and the darker your dyed fabric. The dye does not work as well if the water temperature is below 75° F (24° C) or above 105° F (40° C). **Do not** use water warmer than 105° F (40° C) to dissolve dye powder. *Because some dye colors, particularly yellows, are sensitive to water temperature, I recommend using 95° F (35° C) water to mix dye powder and make dye baths.*

Refer to the table below for optimum water temperatures for dissolving dye and auxiliary products.

Product	Water Temperature		Process
	Fahrenheit	Celsius	
Metaphos (water softener)	75° to 95°	24° to 35°	Add to water
MX Fiber-Reactive Dye	95°	35°	Add water to dye powder
Noniodized table salt	75° to 95°	24° to 35°	Add to water
PRO Dye Activator	110° to 120°	44° to 50°	Add to water
Urea	120°	50°	Add to water
PRO Print Paste Mix SH or F	110° to 120°	44° to 50°	Add to water
PRO Thick SH or F	110° to 120°	44° to 50°	Add to water

Detail of *Gives Me the Hee Bee Gee Bees* by Laura Wasilowski (see page 131).

Dye Concentrate

The following are general directions for mixing dye concentrate (used in immersion dyeing). See the immersion dye-bath recipes on pages 70–84 and/or "Calculating an Immersion Dye Bath for Different Fabrics" on page 40 to determine the quantities of fiber-reactive dye powder and water needed for a specific recipe.

Read through the directions and assemble all the necessary equipment and supplies before you begin. **1**

Equipment

1-cup (250-ml) measure or graduated cylinder
1-quart (1-L) measure, or larger
1-quart (1-L) plastic or glass container
Cellulose sponge, rags, or paper towels
Dust/mist mask or respirator
Measuring cups and spoons or scale
Mixing box (see page 35)
Newspapers
Plastic drop cloth
Rubber gloves
Scissors
Spray bottle filled with water
Stirring tools
Thermometer

Supplies

MX Fiber-Reactive Dye

Helpful Hint

Dissolving Dye Powder

Poorly versus Well-Mixed Concentrate

Mixing dye concentrate is a little like mixing gravy; you want it lump-free! Some dye powders take longer to dissolve than others. When the dye powder is fully dissolved, the concentrate appears translucent. If the concentrate appears opaque or cloudy, the powder is not fully dissolved. If necessary, strain the dye concentrate through several layers of nylon stocking, or add about a tablespoon of urea (12 g) to aid solubility, then strain. Dye powder that is not completely dissolved will not dissolve in the salty water of the dye bath and may leave spots of color on your fabric.

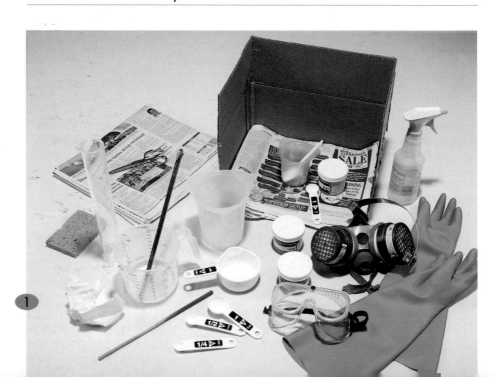

Procedure

1. Cover your work table with the plastic drop cloth.
2. Set the mixing box on top of the drop cloth. Cut a small stack of newspapers to the inside dimensions of the box. Place the news-papers in the bottom of the mixing box and spray them with water. If you spill any of the powder during the mixing process, it will stick to the damp newspaper.
3. Fill the 1-quart (1-L) container half full with warm water. Use this as a rinse container.
4. Fill the 1-cup (250-ml) measure or graduated cylinder with 95° F (35° C) water.
5. Wear a dust/mist mask or respirator and rubber gloves while working with dye powder. Place the container of dye powder in the mixing box. Before opening the container, tap the lid so the powder settles to the bottom. Carefully open the container. Mea-sure level amounts of the powder into a dry 1-quart (1-L) measure. Recap the container.
6. Slowly add enough water to the dye powder to form a smooth paste (make sure all the powder is wet). Stir as you add the water. Move the dye and water aside; then roll up the top layer of newspaper and discard. Once the powder is dissolved, you can put the mixing box away. **2**
7. Gradually add the remaining water. Stir. Once the powder is fully dissolved, it's ready to use. This is the dye concentrate (the basis for the immersion dye bath).
8. Clean up, using the cellulose sponge, rags, or paper towels.

If needed, you can store the dye concentrate at room temperature up to 5 days. I like to mix new concentrate every few days. If the weather is hot and humid, I mix dye concentrate every day.

2

Dye-Stock Solution

The following are general directions for mixing dye-stock solution (used for direct application of dye). You can prepare more or less dye-stock solution according to the amount and type of fabric that you want to dye. One cup (250 ml) of dye-stock solution will color 1½ to 2 yards (1.46 to 1.82 m) of 100% cotton muslin.

Decide whether you want a light, medium, or dark value of the dye color. See the table that follows to determine the amount of dye powder you need.

To make 1 cup (250 ml) of dye-stock solution:

Value	Light		Medium		Dark*	
	English	Metric	English	Metric	English	Metric
MX Fiber-Reactive Dye	½ tsp	1.25 g	2 tsp	5 g	4 to 6 tsp	10 to 15 g

For black, use 10 teaspoons (25 g) per cup of urea water.

Read through the directions and assemble all the necessary equipment and supplies before you begin. ①

Equipment

1-cup (250-ml) measure or graduated cylinder

1-quart (1-L) plastic or glass container

Cellulose sponge, rags, or paper towels

Dust/mist mask or respirator

Measuring cups and spoons or scale

Mixing box (see page 35)

Newspapers

Plastic drop cloth

Rubber gloves

Scissors

Spray bottle filled with water

Stirring tools

Thermometer

Supplies

MX Fiber-Reactive Dye (See the table on the facing page for the amount of dye powder needed.)

1 cup (250 ml) urea water (see pages 52–53)

Procedure

1. Cover your work table with the plastic drop cloth.
2. Set the mixing box on top of the drop cloth. Cut a small stack of newspapers to the inside dimensions of the box. Place the newspapers in the bottom of the mixing box and spray them with water. If you spill any of the powder during the mixing process it will stick to the damp newspaper.
3. Fill the 1-quart (1-L) container half full with warm water. Use this as a rinse container.
4. Wear a dust/mist mask or respirator and rubber gloves while working with dye powder. Before opening the container of dye powder, tap the lid so the powder settles to the bottom. Place the dye powder in the mixing box. Carefully open the container. Measure level amounts of the powder into a dry 1-cup (250-ml) measure. Recap the container.
5. Slowly add enough urea water to the dye powder to form a smooth paste (make sure all the powder is wet). Stir as you add the urea water. Move the dye and urea water aside; then roll up the top layer of newspaper and discard.
6. Gradually add the remaining urea water to the 1-cup (250-ml) mark. Stir. Once the powder is fully dissolved (appears translucent), it's ready to use. This is the dye-stock solution. **2**

7. Clean up, using the cellulose sponge, rags, or paper towels.

If needed, you can store the dye-stock solution at room temperature up to 5 days. I like to mix new solution every few days. If the weather is hot and humid, I mix dye-stock solution every day.

Tips

- Dissolve the dye powder in 95° F (35° C) water. If the dye powder floats on the water and does not mix easily, add a drop of Synthrapol.
- If the dye powder does not mix easily and the concentrate or solution appears cloudy, add a tablespoon (12 g) or more of urea.
- To avoid contaminating dye colors, mix the lightest dye color first; then progress to the darkest color.
- As you work, put dirty utensils in a mayonnaise or yogurt container filled with water.
- After mixing each color, clean and dry your utensils.

Urea Water

For direct-application techniques, fiber-reactive dye powder is mixed with urea water. Urea water helps the dye dissolve and prevents the dye from drying completely during the curing process.

This recipe makes 1 quart (1 L) of urea water. For larger quantities, multiply the ingredients as needed. For example, multiply by 4 to make 1 gallon (4 L).

Read through the directions and assemble all the necessary equipment and supplies before you begin. **1**

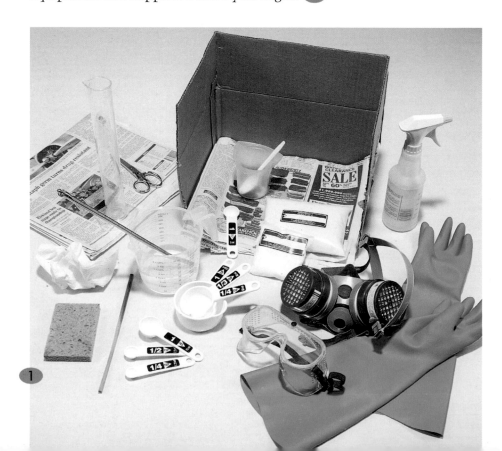

Equipment

Two 1-quart (1-L) measures, or larger

Cellulose sponge, rags, or paper towels

Measuring cup and spoons or scale

Mixing box (see page 35)

Newspapers

Plastic drop cloth

Rubber gloves

Scissors

Spray bottle filled with water

Stirring tools

Thermometer

Supplies

1 teaspoon (7 g) Metaphos (water softener), if needed

1 cup (150 g) urea

Procedure

1. Cover your work table with the plastic drop cloth.
2. Set the mixing box on top of the drop cloth. Cut a small stack of newspapers to the inside dimensions of the box. Place the newspapers in the bottom of the mixing box and spray them with water. If you spill any of the urea during the mixing process it will stick to the damp newspaper.
3. Fill a 1-quart (1-L) measure with 120°F (50°C) water.
4. Pour 3 cups (750 ml) of the water prepared in step 3 into the other 1-quart (1-L) measure.
5. Wear rubber gloves while mixing urea water. Put the container of urea in the mixing box. Carefully open the container. Measure 1 cup (150 g) of urea into the 3 cups (750 ml) of water. Recap the container.
6. Measure 1 teaspoon (7 g) of Metaphos into the 3 cups (750 ml) of water. Stir until both the urea and Metaphos are dissolved (the water will look clear). Urea absorbs heat, so the water will also feel cooler.
7. Add water (from step 3) up to the 1-quart (1-L) mark and stir. Cool the urea water to below 95°F (35°C) before using. You can store the urea water in a closed container at room temperature for approximately 6 months. Discard the urea water if you notice a strong, ammonia-like smell.
8. Clean up, using the cellulose sponge, rags, or paper towels.

Making Activated Urea Water

When I'm working and want to lighten the color of a dye-stock solution for a technique such as hand painting, I add mixed alkali to urea water to make "activated urea water." The mixed alkali is a fixative, and it helps ensure that the diluted dye will not wash off during the rinse process.

Add 1 teaspoon (3 g) of mixed alkali (see page 62) to 1 cup (250 ml) of urea water. Label, date, and store urea water in a closed container at room temperature for approximately two months. Discard the activated urea water if you notice a strong, ammonia-like smell.

Print and Dye Pastes

Print paste is made from water, urea, Metaphos, and seaweed (sodium alginate or PRO Thick SH or F). Purchased print paste has all the ingredients included; you simply add water. Print paste is used to thicken dye-stock solution for direct-application techniques.

Paste consistency is a personal thing; don't be afraid to adjust these recipes. If the dye paste is too thin, thicken it by adding print paste. If the dye paste is too thick, thin it by adding urea water. The consistency that works well for me may not work well for you.

PRINT PASTE FROM A MIX

This recipe makes 1 cup (250 ml) of print paste. Multiply the quantities listed to make larger amounts.

Read through the directions and assemble all the necessary equipment and supplies before you begin. **1**

Equipment

2-cup (500-ml) plastic container or jar
Two 1-cup (250-ml) measures
Cellulose sponge, rags, or paper towels
Measuring cups and spoons or scale
Newspapers
Plastic container or jar with tightly fitting lid (for extra print paste)
Plastic drop cloth
Rubber gloves
Stirring tools
Thermometer

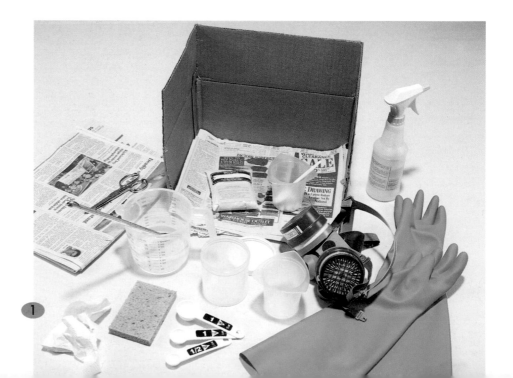

Supplies

5½ tablespoons (55 g) PRO Print Paste Mix SH (see "print paste" on page 38)

Procedure

1. Cover your work area with the plastic drop cloth.
2. Wear rubber gloves while mixing print paste. Measure 5½ tablespoons (55 g) of PRO Print Paste Mix SH into a dry 1-cup (250-ml) measure and set aside.
3. Fill the empty 1-cup (250-ml) container with 110° to 120° F (44° to 50° C) water.
4. Pour ¾ cup (190 ml) of the water prepared in step 3 into the 2-cup (500-ml) measure.
5. Gradually add the PRO Print Paste Mix SH measured in step 2 to the ¾ cup (190 ml) of water while stirring rapidly. Continue stirring until you have a smooth paste. This will take approximately 5 minutes.
6. Add water (from step 3) up to the 1-cup (250-ml) mark and stir until thoroughly mixed. Let stand 1 hour, or overnight for smoothest results.
7. Clean up, using the cellulose sponge, rags, or paper towels.

Label, date, and store unused print paste in a closed container for up to 6 months at room temperature. If you live in a hot and humid climate, you should refrigerate the print paste. (Label your container "Print Paste: Do Not Eat Me.") It is important to let print paste return to room temperature—above 75° F (24° C)—before using.

Over time, print paste changes consistency, becoming thinner. You can still use it for thin dye-paste applications, but discard it if you notice a strong ammonia-like smell.

Helpful Hint

Print paste after 24 hours, 15 minutes, and immediately after mixing; note the differences in consistency. For paste that is smooth and lump-free, mix it the day before you plan to use it.

Making Activated Print Paste

When I'm working and want to lighten the color of a dye paste, I add mixed alkali to the print paste to make "activated print paste." Mixed alkali is a fixative that keeps the dye from washing off during the rinse process.

Add 1 teaspoon (3 g) of mixed alkali (see pages 62–63) to 1 cup (250 ml) of prepared print paste. Stir.

Label, date, and store activated print paste in a closed container for up to two months at room temperature. If you live in a hot and humid climate, you should refrigerate the print paste. (Label: "Activated Print Paste: Do Not Eat Me.") It is important to let print paste return to room temperature—above 75° F (24° C)—before using. Discard it if you notice a strong ammonia-like smell.

PRINT PASTE FROM SCRATCH

This recipe makes 1 cup (250 ml) of print paste. For paste that is smooth and lump-free, mix the print paste the day before you plan to use it.

Read through the directions and assemble all the necessary equipment and supplies before you begin. **1**

Equipment

2-cup (500-ml) measure

Two 1-cup (250-ml) measures

Cellulose sponge, rags, or paper towels

Measuring cups and spoons or scale

Mixing box (see page 35)

Newspapers

Plastic container or jar with tightly fitting lid (for extra print paste)

Plastic drop cloth

Rubber gloves

Scissors

Spray bottle filled with water

Stirring tools

Thermometer

Supplies

¼ teaspoon (1.75 g) Metaphos (water softener)

1 teaspoon (3 g) PRO Thick SH (see "print paste" on page 38)

10 teaspoons (40 g) urea

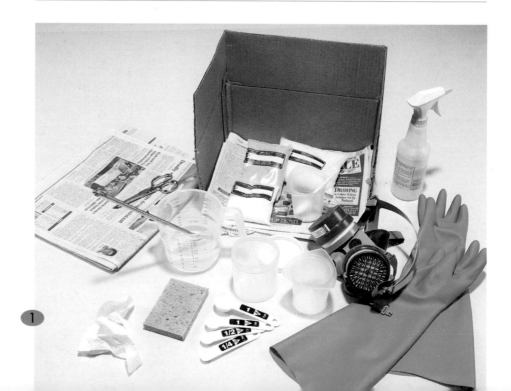

1

Procedure

1. Cover your work table with the plastic drop cloth.

2. Set the mixing box on top of the drop cloth. Cut a small stack of newspapers to the inside dimensions of the box. Place the newspapers in the bottom of the mixing box and spray them with water. If you spill any of the powder during the mixing process it will stick to the damp newspaper.

3. Wear rubber gloves while mixing print paste. Measure 1 teaspoon (3 g) of PRO Thick SH into a dry 1-cup (250-ml) measure and set aside.

4. Fill the empty 1-cup (250-ml) container with 110° to 120° F (44° to 50° C) water.

5. Pour ¾ cup (190 ml) of the water prepared in step 4 into the 2-cup (500-ml) measure.

6. Put the container of urea in the mixing box. Carefully open the container. Measure 6 teaspoons (40 g) of urea into the ¾ cup (190 ml) of water. Recap the container.

7. Measure ¼ teaspoon (1.75 g) of Metaphos into the ¾ cup (190 ml) of water. Stir until both the urea and Metaphos are dissolved (the water will look clear). Urea absorbs heat, so the water will also feel cooler.

8. Gradually add 1 teaspoon (3 g) of PRO Thick SH to the ¾ cup (190 ml) of water while stirring rapidly. Continue stirring until you have a smooth paste. This will take approximately 5 minutes.

9. Add water (from step 4) up to the 1-cup (250-ml) mark and stir until thoroughly mixed. Let stand 1 hour or overnight for smoothest results.

10. Clean up, using the cellulose sponge, rags, or paper towels.

You can store unused print paste in a closed container for up to 6 months at room temperature. If you live in a hot and humid climate, you should refrigerate the print paste. (Label it "Print Paste: Do Not Eat Me.") It is important to let print paste return to room temperature—above 75° F (24° C)—before using.

Over time, prepared print paste changes consistency, becoming thinner. You can still use old print paste for thin dye-paste applications, but discard it if you notice a strong ammonia-like smell.

DYE PASTE

Dye paste is a mixture of fiber-reactive dye powder, urea water, and prepared print paste. Thin dye paste flows easily and is ideal for hand painting. Thick dye paste holds a line and stays where you place it, without bleeding around the edges, making it ideal for monoprinting, stenciling, and stamping. Whether your dye paste is thin or thick depends on how much print paste you add.

Print paste is an "antimigrant," meaning it inhibits dye from spreading and penetrating the fabric. Therefore, it is important to use only as much print paste as you need. Make the dye paste as thin as possible for the desired application. Different consistencies work best with different fabrics. Thin dye paste, the consistency of heavy cream, works best on heavy fabric. Thick dye paste, the consistency of honey, works best on lightweight fabric.

If the dye paste is too thin, thicken it by adding print paste. If the dye paste is too thick, thin it by adding urea water.

This recipe makes 1 cup (250 ml) of dye paste. You can prepare more or less dye paste according to the amount of fabric you want to dye. One cup of dye paste will generally color 1½ to 2 yards (1.46 to 1.82 m) of 100% cotton muslin, depending on the recipe.

Read through the directions and assemble all the necessary equipment and supplies before you begin. **1**

Equipment

1-quart (1-L) plastic or glass container
Two 1-cup (250-ml) measures or graduated cylinders
Cellulose sponge, rags, or paper towels

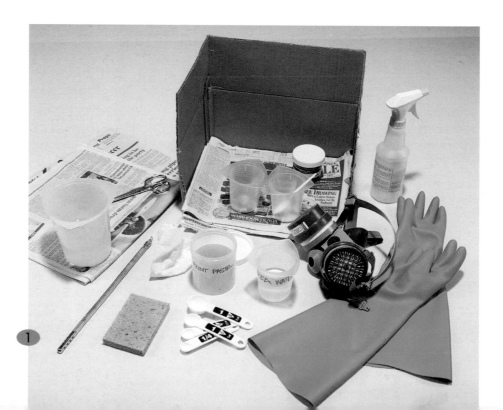

1

Dust/mist mask or respirator

Measuring cups and spoons or scale

Mixing box (see page 35)

Newspapers

Plastic container or jar with tightly fitting lid (for extra dye paste)

Plastic drop cloth

Rubber gloves

Scissors

Spray bottle filled with water

Stirring tools

Thermometer

Supplies

½ to 6 teaspoons (1.25 to 15 g) MX Fiber-Reactive Dye*

1 teaspoon to 1 cup (5 to 250 ml) print paste (see pages 54–57)*

2 tablespoons to 1 cup (30 to 250 ml) urea water (see pages 52–53)*

*Quantity depends on the thickness desired, as explained in the directions that follow.

Procedure

1. Cover your work table with the plastic drop cloth.
2. Set the mixing box on top of the drop cloth. Cut a small stack of newspapers to the inside dimensions of the box. Place the newspapers in the bottom of the mixing box and spray them with water. If you spill any of the powder during the mixing process it will stick to the damp newspaper.
3. Fill the 1-quart (1-L) container half full with warm water. Use this as a rinse container.
4. Decide whether you want to make a light, medium, or dark value of the dye color. See the following table to determine the amount of dye powder you need. Wear a dust/mist mask or respirator and rubber gloves while working with dye powder. Place one of the 1-cup (250-ml) measures in the mixing box. Mix the dye powder with just enough urea water to make a lump-free paste.

To make 1 cup (250 ml) of dye paste:

Value	Light		Medium		Dark*	
	English	Metric	English	Metric	English	Metric
MX Fiber-Reactive Dye	½ tsp	1.25 g	2 tsp	5 g	4 to 6 tsp	10 to 15 g

*For black, use 10 teaspoons (25 g) per cup of dye paste.

5. **To make thin dye paste,** mix 1 to 2 teaspoons (5 to 10 ml) of the prepared print paste with the paste mixed in step 4. Add urea water to make 1 cup (250 ml). Stir until thoroughly mixed. Thin dye paste is ideal for hand painting.

   To make thick dye paste, add prepared print paste to the paste mixed in step 4 to make 1 cup (250 ml). Stir until thoroughly mixed. Thick dye paste is ideal for monoprinting, stenciling, and stamping.

6. Clean up, using the cellulose sponge, rags, or paper towels.

   If needed, you can store the dye paste at room temperature up to 5 days. I like to mix new dye paste every few days. If the weather is hot and humid, I mix dye paste every day.

Activator Soak and Mixed Alkali

There are several ways to fix or "cure" (permanently set) dye when you use a direct-application technique. This book focuses on the two most popular methods: activator soak and mixed alkali. In each direct-application recipe, I recommend one curing method or the other based on how easy it is to use, how long the dye needs to react with the fiber, and how easy it is to wash out. However, you can use either of these methods. I encourage you to try both to determine which works best for you. Here are a few helpful guidelines:

- If you need several days to complete a project, it will be easiest to prepare the fabric with activator soak. Once you have added fixative (mixed alkali) to the dye paste, you must use it within 4 hours. But, if you have not added fixative, you can use the dye paste for up to 5 days.

- If you plan to apply many layers of dye, you will get the best results using the mixed-alkali method. By mixing the fixative with the dye, you are assured of having enough fixing agent to

set the dye. Also, if your design has areas that you don't want to pattern, there is less chance of "back printing," or staining, the light areas during rinsing and washing.

ACTIVATOR SOAK

Activator soak is a mixture of PRO Dye Activator and water. This mixture pre-fixes the fabric so the dye reacts with the fibers when it is applied. You can soak cotton fabric just prior to dyeing or up to two months in advance. Fabric that is treated just before dyeing seems to yield brighter colors than fabric that has been treated and stored for a long time.

Fabric prepared in advance should be air dried. Use a cool iron to touch up any wrinkles. Do not use a hot iron; fabric treated with activator scorches easily. Unfortunately, scorch marks usually do not come out. Treated cotton tends to turn yellow if it is stored for a long time. This color change is usually permanent.

You can also prepare silk in activator soak, but you should dye it within 2 weeks. The pH of the activator is high, and the silk will begin to deteriorate if the activator is not neutralized.

This recipe makes 1 gallon (4 L) of activator soak. You can prepare more or less according to the amount of fabric you want to dye. It is important that the fabric be able to move freely while soaking.

Read through the directions and assemble all the necessary equipment and supplies before you begin. ①

Equipment

1-quart (1-L) measure, or larger
2-gallon (8-L) plastic bucket, or larger, with tightly fitting lid
Cellulose sponge, rags, or paper towels
Dust/mist mask or respirator
Measuring cups and spoons or scale
Mixing box (see page 35)
Newspapers
Plastic drop cloth
Rubber gloves
Scissors
Spray bottle filled with water
Stirring tools
Thermometer

Supplies

9 tablespoons (80 g) PRO Dye Activator (see "activator" on page 37)

Procedure

1. Cover your work table with the plastic drop cloth.
2. Set the mixing box on top of the drop cloth. Cut a small stack of newspapers to the inside dimensions of the box. Place the newspapers in the bottom of the mixing box and spray them with water. If you spill any of the powder during the mixing process it will stick to the damp newspaper.
3. Put the bucket in the mixing box.
4. Measure 1 gallon (4 L) of 110° to 120° F (44° to 50° C) water into the bucket. (If you are using a 1-quart measure, 4 quarts makes a gallon.)
5. Wear a dust/mist mask or respirator and rubber gloves while working with activator powder. Add 9 tablespoons (80 g) of activator powder to the bucket. Stir until dissolved.
6. Clean up, using the cellulose sponge, rags, or paper towels.

Label and date the bucket of activator soak. You can store activator soak at room temperature, in a bucket with a tightly fitting lid, for 6 to 8 months.

MIXED ALKALI

Mixed alkali is a mixture of PRO Dye Activator and baking soda. This dry mixture is added directly to the dye-stock solution or paste, which is then applied to fabric. Once you have added mixed alkali to the dye, you must use it within four hours. You may want to write the expiration time on the side of the dye-stock solution or paste container. This way, you'll never labor over a design that will wash out!

Read through the directions and assemble all the necessary equipment and supplies before you begin. **1**

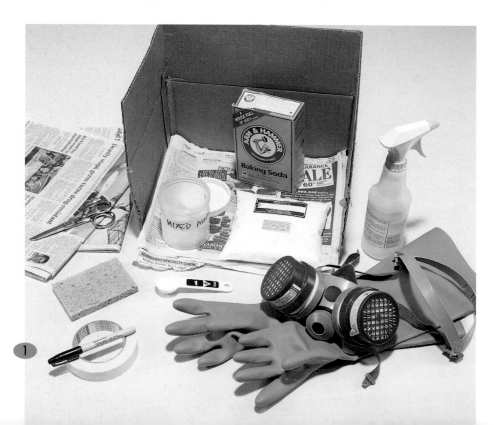

Equipment

4- to 8-ounce (114- to 228-g) wide-mouth container with tightly fitting lid

Cellulose sponge, rags, or paper towels

Dust/mist mask or respirator

Measuring spoons or scale

Mixing box (see page 35)

Newspapers

Plastic drop cloth

Rubber gloves

Scissors

Spray bottle filled with water

Supplies

4 tablespoons (48 g) baking soda

1 tablespoon (9 g) PRO Dye Activator (see "activator" on page 37)

Procedure

1. Cover your work table with the plastic drop cloth.
2. Set the mixing box on top of the drop cloth. Cut a small stack of newspapers to the inside dimensions of the box. Place the newspapers in the bottom of the mixing box and spray them with water. If you spill any of the powder during the mixing process it will stick to the damp newspaper.
3. Wear a dust/mist mask or respirator and rubber gloves while working with activator powder. Put the wide-mouth container in the mixing box. Measure 4 tablespoons (48 g) of baking soda and 1 tablespoon (9 g) of PRO Dye Activator into the wide-mouth container. Cap the container; then shake until well blended.
4. Clean up, using the cellulose sponge, rags, or paper towels.

Label, date, and store the mixed alkali in a cool, dry place. Discard after 6 months. (Label the container "Mixed Alkali: Do Not Eat Me.")

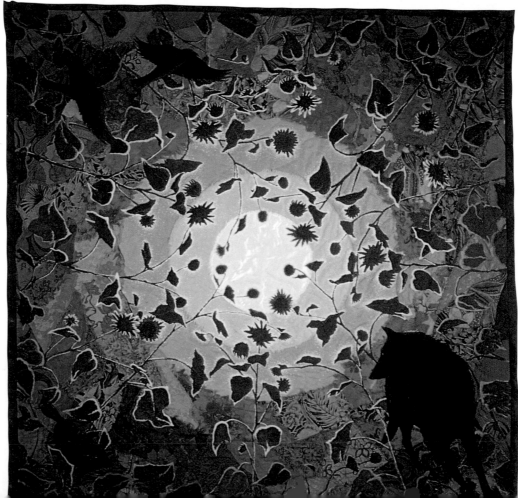

▶ *The Wind Does Not Require the Grass to Answer*
by Roxana Bartlett, 1994, Boulder, Colorado, 69" x 69". **Method**: Mixed-media quilt. Fiber-reactive dye and textile paint on cotton, rayon, and wool. Machine pieced, hand appliquéd, and hand quilted. Photo by Ken Sanville.

▼ *Soft Stirs the New of Light*
by Roxana Bartlett, 1992, Boulder, Colorado, 69" x 69". **Method**: Mixed-media quilt. Fiber-reactive dye and textile paint on cotton, rayon, and wool. Machine pieced and hand appliquéd and quilted. Photo by Ken Sanville.

▲ *Epiphany*
by Gabrielle Swain, 1995, Watauga, Texas, 58" x 77". **Method:** Fiber-reactive dye on cotton. Hand pieced and quilted. Photo by Brent Kane.

◄ *Life in the Margin #8*
by Caryl Bryer Fallert, 1996, Oswego, Illinios, 23" x 23". **Method:** Fiber-reactive dye on cotton. Hand painted. Machine appliquéd and quilted. Photo by the artist.

▲ *Moonstruck*
by Melody Johnson, 1997, Cary, Illinois, 60½" x 80".
Method: Fiber-reactive dye on cotton. Hand appliquéd
and machine quilted. Photo by the artist.

∧ *Drawn to Edges ... Cape Newagen*
by Gayle Fraas and Duncan Slade, 1994, Edgecomb,
Maine, 60" x 60". **Method**: Whole-cloth quilt. Fiber-
reactive dye on cotton. Hand painted. Machine and
hand quilted by the artists. Photo by Dennis Griggs.

< Detail of *Drawn to Edges ... Cape Newagen*

➚ *32 Warwick*
by Heather Allen, 1997, Asheville, North Carolina, 36" x 75".
Method: Fiber-reactive dye and textile paint on cotton. Machine pieced and quilted and hand beaded.
Photo by Tim Barnwell.

➚ *Fire on the Lake*
by L. Carlene Raper, 1993, Putney, Vermont, 83" x 102".
Method: Fiber-reactive dye on cotton. Machine pieced and tied.
Photo by Jim Thomas.

◁ *Dance in Several Sections*
by Astrid Hilger Bennett, 1991, Iowa City, Iowa, 55" x 65".
Method: Fiber-reactive dye on cotton duck. Hand painted. Machine quilted. Photo by the artist.

∧ *Summer Beach I*
by Astrid Hilger Bennett, 1996,
Iowa City, Iowa, 76" x 42".
Method: Fiber-reactive dye on
cotton. Machine pieced and
quilted. Photo by the artist.

‹ *No Thistles in My
Garden: Hiroshima Series*
by Barbara Moll, 1996,
Muncie, Indiana, 39" x 47".
Method: Whole-cloth quilt.
Fiber-reactive dye on cotton.
Hand printed and painted.
Machine quilted. Photo by
Joan Whitaker.

Immersion Dye Techniques

Immersion dyeing, also called "vat" or "exhaust" dyeing, is the most efficient method for creating a solid-colored fabric. Fabric is submerged in warm water with dye and auxiliary products for sixty to ninety minutes (with periodic stirring for even color). After the fabric has soaked for the allotted time, it is rinsed to remove excess fixative, washed, and dried. There are several tricks to successful immersion dyeing:

- Don't worry if the dye bath changes color during dyeing. Both the dye bath and the fabric may change colors several times as the different dyes "strike" or are absorbed by the fabric.
- If you dye different types of fabric in the same dye bath, the fabrics will dye different colors (or shades of the same color) based on which fabric is more absorbent.
- Be sure to dye your fabric for the full sixty to ninety minutes (refer to the specific recipe). Shortening the dye bath causes "surface dyeing"—the dye does not fully penetrate the fiber. Surface-dyed fabrics are neither lightfast nor washfast. Also, shortening the dye bath prevents mixed colors from being absorbed by fabric and will probably affect your desired color. *Different dye colors strike (are absorbed by and react with) the fiber at different times during the dye bath.*
- Remember that the color of the dried, dyed fabric will be lighter than the color of the wet, dyed fabric. Think about wet versus dry blue jeans. As you gain experience, you will learn to evaluate wet fabric color.
- Be sure to keep a detailed record book (see page 35) of your dyeing, including your disappointments. The more information you gather and experience you gain, the more comfortable you will be mixing colors and predicting results!

This section includes recipes for a basic immersion dye bath, an immersion dye bath in a washing machine, a value gradation, a hue gradation, and resist techniques for immersion dyeing. Review "Protecting Yourself and Your Environment" on pages 16–17 for guidelines on working with dye and auxiliary powders.

USING A BASIC DYE BATH

This recipe will dye 1 yard (91 cm) of 100% cotton muslin a medium value of 1 color. Preparation, dyeing, and cleanup takes approximately 2 hours. (It may take longer if you are not familiar with the immersion dye bath process.) Remember to wear rubber gloves when you work with the fabric in the dye bath.

Read through the directions, and assemble the equipment and supplies before you begin. Wear a dust/mist mask or respirator while working with dye powder and auxiliary products. **1**

Equipment

1-cup (250-ml) measure or graduated cylinder

1-quart (1-L) measure, or larger

2-gallon (8-L) plastic bucket, or larger, for dye bath

Cellulose sponge, rags, or paper towels

Clothesline and clothespins (optional)

Dust/mist mask or respirator

Kitchen timer or watch

Measuring cups and spoons or scale

Mixing box (see page 35)

Newspapers

Plastic drop cloth

Rubber gloves

Spray bottle filled with water

Stirring tools

Thermometer

Immersion-Dyed Fabric

Supplies

²/₃ cup (180 g) noniodized table salt

³/₈ teaspoon (2.3 g) Metaphos, if you have hard water

1³/₄ teaspoons (4.5 g) MX Fiber-Reactive Dye
(see "Color Mixing" on pages 41–45)

5 teaspoons (15 g) PRO Dye Activator

1 yard (91 cm) scoured, 100% cotton muslin (see pages 22–24)

¼ teaspoon (1.25 ml) Synthrapol (minimum)

Helpful Hint

Level Dyeing

For "level" dyeing (even color), stir, stir, stir! Rearrange the fabric folds often during the immersion dye-bath process, and make sure the fabric can move freely in the dye bath.

Procedure

1. Cover your work table with the plastic drop cloth. If your scoured fabric is dry, soak it in 1 gallon (4 L) of 110° F (44° C) water with ¼ teaspoon (1.25 ml) of Synthrapol for 10 to 15 minutes.

2. Pour 3 quarts (3 L) of 95° F (35° C) water into the 2-gallon (8-L) plastic bucket. This bucket will contain the dye bath.

3. Add ½ cup (180 g) of salt. Stir until dissolved.

4. If you have hard water, add ⅜ teaspoon (2.3 g) of Metaphos. Stir until dissolved.

5. Following the instructions for mixing dye concentrate on pages 48–50, dissolve 1¾ teaspoons (4.5 g) of dye powder in 1 cup (250 ml) of 95° F (35° C) water. Pour this into the bucket to complete the dye bath.

6. Make sure the fabric is completely wet before adding it to the dye bath. If you are not sure that the fabric is completely wet, add ¼ teaspoon (1.25 ml) of Synthrapol to the dye bath before adding the fabric.

7. Add the wet fabric to the dye bath. Stir to make sure that there are no air bubbles trapped in the fabric. Set the timer for 15 minutes. Stir the fabric intermittently, rearranging the folds. ①

8. To mix the fixative, dissolve 5 teaspoons (15 g) of PRO Dye Activator in ½ cup (125 ml) of 110° to 120° F (44° to 50° C) water. Set aside.

9. When the timer rings, remove the fabric from the dye bath and set it aside in the empty bucket. Pour the fixative prepared in step 8 into the dye bath and stir. *Don't worry if the dye bath changes color when you add the fixative; it will not affect the final color of your fabric.* ②

10. Return the fabric to the dye bath and set the timer for 60 minutes. Stir the fabric continuously for the first 15 minutes, rearranging the folds; then stir every 5 minutes until the timer rings. Stirring at this stage is very important for level dyeing. Make sure to rearrange the folds frequently.

11. When the timer rings, remove the fabric and pour the dye bath down the drain. Dye baths cannot be stored or reused after the fixative has been added.

12. To rinse and wash the fabric by hand, put it in the empty dye bucket and fill the bucket half full with 65° to 75° F (18° to 24° C) water. Swish the fabric around for a minute or so; then pour the rinse water down the drain. Repeat this process, changing the rinse water three or four times. When the fabric feels squeaky clean (not soapy), remove it and empty the rinse bucket. (It's okay for the rinse water to be colored.) Refill the bucket with 140° F (60° C) water. Add ¼ teaspoon (1.25 ml) of Synthrapol and stir. Return the fabric to the rinse bucket and swish it around for 5 minutes. Rinse the fabric in warm (comfortable to the touch) water.

To rinse and wash the fabric by machine, set your washing machine on the small load, warm wash, and warm rinse cycles. After the machine fills and begins to agitate, add the fabric. Close the lid and let the machine continue through the wash, rinse, and spin cycles. After the final spin cycle, reset the machine on the hot wash and warm rinse cycles. After the machine fills with water, add ¼ teaspoon (1.25 ml) of Synthrapol for each yard of fabric and let the machine continue through all the cycles. Check the last rinse cycle. If the rinse water is colored, you may need to repeat this step. For dark colors, 2 short wash treatments may work better than 1 long wash.

13. Dry the fabric in a clothes dryer or on a clothesline. Follow the dryer manufacturer's instructions for the appropriate heat setting.

14. Clean up, using cellulose sponge, rags, or paper towels.

USING A WASHING MACHINE

Washing-machine dyeing is a good technique to use when you want to dye a large amount of fabric a solid color. This technique takes much of the physical work out of the immersion dye bath process. You can dye up to 15 yards (13.6 m) of fabric in an extra-large capacity, top-loading washing machine in 2 to 2½ hours!

For different amounts of fabric, increase or decrease the quantities of dye, auxiliary products, and water. (See "Calculating an Immersion Dye Bath for Different Fabrics" on page 40.) To adjust the amount of water, set your washing machine for small, medium, large, or extra-large loads.

I recommend cutting your fabric into lengths of no more than 4 to 5 yards (3.6 to 4.5 m) each. When working with fabric pieces that are 4 yards or longer, check the fabric frequently during the dye cycle to make sure it is not twisted. Dye cannot evenly penetrate twisted fabric. If the fabric does twist, unwind it during the 5-minute stop cycles (step 6). Remember to wear rubber gloves when you work with the fabric in the dye bath.

Read through the directions, and assemble the equipment and supplies before you begin. Wear a dust/mist mask or respirator while working with dye powder and auxiliary products.

Equipment

2-quart (2-L) measure, or larger
Cellulose sponge, rags, or paper towels
Clothesline and clothespins (optional)
Dust/mist mask or respirator
Kitchen timer or watch
Measuring cups and spoons or scale
Mixing box (see page 35)

Helpful Hint

Preventing Spotty Dyeing

Always remove your fabric before adding activator to the dye bath. Stir well before and after you return the fabric to prevent spotty dyeing.

| Newspapers |
| Nylon stocking or cheesecloth (optional) |
| Plastic drop cloth |
| Rubber gloves |
| Spray bottle filled with water |
| Stirring tools |
| Thermometer |
| Washing machine |

Helpful Hint

Cleaning your Washing Machine

I have not stained any laundry after using my washing machine for dyeing. After dyeing fabric in your washing machine, wipe the outside of your machine with a damp cloth to mop up any spilled dye. The rinse and wash cycles clean the inside of the machine.

Supplies

The amount of each ingredient needed is based on the weight of the fabric and the value of the dye color. Refer to the table that follows.

| Up to 15 yards (13.6 m) 100% cotton muslin |
| Metaphos, if you have hard water |
| MX Fiber-Reactive Dye (see "Color Mixing" on pages 41–45) |
| Noniodized table salt |
| PRO Dye Activator |
| Synthrapol |

For 5 pounds (2.3 kg) of dry fabric—approximately 15 yards (14 m) of 100% cotton muslin—use the following amounts. If your fabric weighs more or less than 5 pounds, refer to page 40.

Value	Light		Medium		Dark*	
	English	Metric	English	Metric	English	Metric
Metaphos	5 tsp	35 g	5 tsp	35 g	5 tsp	35 g
MX Fiber-Reactive Dye	5 tsp	13 g	7½ Tbl	68 g	15 Tbl	136 g
Noniodized Table Salt	6 cups	1.8 kg	9 cups	2.72 kg	12 cups	3.6 kg
PRO Dye Activator	¾ cup	115 g	1½ cups	230 g	2¼ cups	345 g

For black, double the amount of dye powder and extend the dyeing time to 90 minutes (after adding activator).

Procedure

1. Cover your work area with the plastic drop cloth.
2. Weigh the dry fabric (see page 40). Use the weight of the fabric to determine the exact amount of each ingredient needed.
3. When you use your washing machine to dye large amounts of fabric, it is best to scour (pages 23–24) all the fabric in the machine before preparing the dye bath. Machine wash the fabric on the extra-large load, hot cycle—minimum temperature 140° F (60° C)—with ¼ teaspoon (1 g) of PRO Dye Activator and

¼ teaspoon (1.25 ml) of Synthrapol per yard (91 cm) of dry fabric. After the rinse cycle, remove the wet fabric and set it aside while you prepare the dye bath.

4. Set your washing machine on the extra-large load, warm wash, and warm rinse cycles. The water temperature should be 95° F (35° C). Remove 2 quarts (2 L) of water from the machine and set aside. After the machine fills and begins to agitate, add the salt and Metaphos (if needed) indicated in the chart. Let the machine agitate until the salt dissolves; then stop the wash cycle.

5. Refer to the preceding table to determine the amount of dye powder you need. Following the instructions for mixing dye concentrate on pages 48–50, dissolve the dye powder in the water set aside in step 3; then pour it into the washing machine. Let the machine agitate until the dye is thoroughly mixed; then stop the wash cycle.

6. Add the wet fabric, distributing it evenly around the tub. Start the machine and set the timer for 15 minutes. If the wash cycle ends before the 15 minutes are up, stop the machine. Wait 5 to 10 minutes, then restart the wash cycle so the dye bath does not go down the drain. When the timer rings, stop the wash cycle. During the wash cycle, check the fabric frequently to make sure it is not twisted.

7. Refer to the preceding table to determine the amount of PRO Dye Activator you need. To make the fixative, dissolve the activator separately in 2 quarts (2 L) of 110° to 120° F (44° to 50° C) water.

   If your washing machine has a spout for liquid bleach, pour 2 cups (500 ml) of the fixative through the spout. Restart the machine and set the timer for 5 minutes. When the timer rings, add another 2 cups (500 ml) of the fixative through the liquid-bleach spout and set the timer for 5 minutes. When the timer rings, add the remaining fixative and set the timer for 5 minutes. Remember to reset the machine so the dye bath does not go down the drain.

   If your washing machine does not have a liquid-bleach spout, slowly pour all the fixative into the machine while it is agitating. Do not pour the fixative directly on the fabric; this causes uneven dyeing.

8. When the timer rings, stop the machine and let the fabric sit for 5 minutes. Restart the machine and agitate the fabric for another 5 minutes. Repeat this process for 60 minutes. Adjust your washing machine as necessary (to agitate only) so the dye bath does not go down the drain.

9. At the end of 60 minutes, let the machine continue through the wash, rinse, and spin cycles. After the final spin cycle, reset the machine to the hot wash and warm rinse cycles. Allow the washing machine to fill with water. The water temperature for the hot wash should be 140° F (60° C).

Dealing with Undissolved Dye

If you are not sure that the dye is thoroughly dissolved, strain the dye concentrate through several layers of nylon stocking before pouring it into the washing machine.

After the machine fills with water, add ¼ teaspoon (1.25 ml) of Synthrapol per yard (91 cm) of fabric and let the machine continue through all the cycles. Check the last rinse cycle. If the rinse water is colored, you may need to repeat this step.

10. Dry the fabric in a clothes dryer or on a clothesline. Follow the dryer manufacturer's instructions for the appropriate heat setting.

11. Clean up, using the cellulose sponge, rags, or paper towels.

DYEING A VALUE GRADATION

A value gradation—a progression of values, lightest to darkest, of one color—creates an appealing visual rhythm. Use this recipe to dye a value gradation with 6 even steps—¼ yard (23 cm) of each value. Keep in mind that the more dye baths you use, the longer setup and cleanup will take. Remember to wear rubber gloves when you work with the fabric in the dye bath.

Read through the directions, and assemble the equipment and supplies before you begin. Wear a dust/mist mask or respirator while working with dye powder and auxiliary products.

Six-Step Value Gradation Fabrics

Equipment

1-quart (1-L) plastic container or jar
6 plastic cups (empty yogurt or margarine tubs)
6 long-handled spoons or assorted stirring tools
Seven 1-gallon (4-L) plastic buckets
Cellulose sponge, rags, or paper towels
Clothesline and clothespins (optional)
Dust/mist mask or respirator
Kitchen timer or watch
Marking pen
Masking tape
Measuring cups and spoons or scale
Mixing box (see page 35)
Newspapers
Plastic drop cloth
Plastic or Styrofoam plates
Rubber gloves
Scissors
Spray bottle filled with water
Thermometer

Supplies

1½ teaspoons (10.5 g) Metaphos, if you have hard water	
2 teaspoons (5 g) MX Fiber-Reactive Dye (see "Color Mixing" on pages 41–45)	
1½ cups (270 g) noniodized table salt	
¼ cup (27 g) PRO Dye Activator	
1½ yards (1.46 m) scoured, 100% cotton muslin (see page 22)	
¼ teaspoon (1.25 g) Synthrapol (minimum)	

Procedure

1. Cover your work table with the plastic drop cloth.
2. Cut the fabric into 6 fat quarters, 18" x 22" (46 cm x 56 cm), or 6 long quarters, 9" x 44" (23 cm x 112 cm). If your scoured fabric is dry, soak it in 1 gallon (4 L) of 110° F (44° C) water with ¼ teaspoon (1.25 g) of Synthrapol for 10 to 15 minutes.
3. Fill 1 plastic bucket half full with warm water. Use this as a rinse bucket to wash your gloved hands between additions to each dye bath.
4. Label the remaining plastic buckets with masking tape. Number them 1–6. Place the buckets in numerical order, from left to right, on your work table. Place a spoon in each of the 6 buckets.
5. Pour 3½ cups (875 ml) of 95° F (35° C) water into each bucket.
6. Add ¼ cup (45 g) of salt to each bucket. Stir until dissolved.
7. If you have hard water, add ¼ teaspoon (1.2 g) of Metaphos to each bucket. Stir until dissolved.
8. Following the instructions for mixing dye concentrate on pages 48–50, dissolve 2 teaspoons (5 g) of dye powder in 1 cup (250 ml) of 95° F (35° C) water.

   You may want to experiment with the amount of dye powder. For darker values, use 3 to 4 teaspoons (7.5 to 10 g) of dye powder. For lighter values, use 1 teaspoon (2.5 g) of dye powder.
9. Fill the 1-quart (1-L) container with 95° F (35° C) water.
10. Measure the dye concentrate into the buckets as follows:
    Bucket #1: Pour ½ cup (125 ml) of the dye concentrate into bucket #1 and stir. ①

Buckets #2–#5: Using the water from the container you filled in step 9, refill the dye-concentrate cup to the 1-cup (250-ml) mark. Pour ½ cup (125 ml) of the diluted dye concentrate into bucket #2 and stir. Repeat this process for buckets #3, #4, and #5, continuing to dilute the dye concentrate.

Bucket #6: Using the water from the container you filled in step 9, refill the dye-concentrate cup to the 1-cup (250-ml) mark. Pour ½ cup (125 ml) of the diluted dye concentrate into bucket #6 and stir. Discard the remaining ½ cup (125 ml) of dye concentrate.

11. To make the fixative, dissolve ¼ cup (27 g) of PRO Dye Activator in 1½ cups (375 ml) of 120° F (50° C) water. Use the 1-quart (1-L) container for mixing.

12. Measure ¼ cup (63 ml) of the fixative into each of the 6 plastic cups. Place one plastic cup in front of each dye bath.

13. Make sure all the fabric is completely wet before adding it to the dye baths. If you are not sure that the fabric is completely wet, add ¼ teaspoon (1 ml) of Synthrapol to each dye bath before adding the fabric.

14. Add a piece of wet fabric to each dye bath. Set the timer for 15 minutes. Stir the fabric in each dye bath for about 30 seconds, beginning with bucket #1 and ending with bucket #6. Make sure there are no air bubbles trapped in the fabric, and rearrange the folds as you stir. Repeat this process until the timer rings.

    If you use your gloved hands to stir the fabric, make sure to rinse them in the bucket prepared in step 3 before proceeding to the next dye bath.

15. When the timer rings, remove the fabric from bucket #1 and set it aside on a plastic plate. Pour the fixative from the plastic cup into the dye bath and stir. Return the fabric and stir. Repeat this process for all the dye baths, rinsing your gloved hands before proceeding to the next dye bath. **2**

2

16. Set the timer for 60 minutes. Stir the fabric in each dye bath for about 30 seconds, beginning with bucket #1 and ending with bucket #6. Repeat this process for 15 minutes, then once every 5 minutes until the timer rings. Stirring at this stage is very important for level dyeing. Rearrange the folds frequently.

17. When the timer rings, carry each bucket to a sink and remove the fabric. Pour the dye bath down the drain and put the fabric back in the empty bucket.

18. To rinse and wash the fabric by hand, fill each bucket half full with 65° to 75° F (18° to 24° C) water. Swish the fabric around for a minute or so; then pour the rinse water down the drain. Rinse again. Repeat this process for each bucket. After the first 2 rinses, put all the fabric in 1 bucket and repeat the rinse process at least twice. When the fabric feels squeaky clean (not soapy), remove it and empty the rinse bucket. (It's okay for the rinse water to be colored.) Refill the bucket with 140° F (60° C) water. Add ¼ teaspoon (1.25 ml) of Synthrapol per yard of fabric. Return the fabric to the rinse bucket and swish it around for 5 minutes. Rinse the fabric in warm (comfortable to the touch) water.

    To rinse and wash the fabric by machine, set your washing machine on the small load, warm wash, and warm rinse cycles. Wring out each piece of fabric. After the machine fills and begins to agitate, add the fabric. Distribute it evenly around the tub. Close the lid and let the machine continue through the wash, rinse, and spin cycles. After the final spin cycle, reset the machine on the hot wash and warm rinse cycles. After the machine fills with water, add ¼ teaspoon (1.25 ml) of Synthrapol per yard of fabric and let the machine continue through all the cycles. Check the last rinse cycle. If the rinse water is colored, you may need to repeat this step. For dark colors, 2 short wash treatments may work better than 1 long wash.

19. Dry the fabric in a clothes dryer or on a clothesline. Follow the dryer manufacturer's instructions for the appropriate heat setting.

20. Clean up, using a cellulose sponge, rags, or paper towels.

Six-Step Hue Gradation Fabrics

DYEING A HUE GRADATION

A hue gradation is a smooth transition from one color to another. Use this recipe to create striking colors while dyeing a 6-step hue gradation—¼ yard (23 cm) of each hue. Keep in mind that the more dye baths you use, the longer setup and cleanup will take. Remember to wear rubber gloves when you work with the fabric in the dye bath.

Read through the directions, and assemble the equipment and supplies before you begin. Wear a dust/mist mask or respirator while working with dye powder and auxiliary products.

Equipment

1-quart (1-L) plastic container or jar

6 plastic cups (empty yogurt or margarine tubs)

6 long-handled spoons or assorted stirring tools

Seven 1-gallon (4-L) plastic buckets

Cellulose sponge, rags, or paper towels

Clothesline and clothespins (optional)

Dust/mist mask or respirator

Kitchen timer or watch

Marking pen

Masking tape

Measuring cups and spoons or scale

Mixing box (see page 35)

Newspapers

Plastic drop cloth

Plastic or Styrofoam plates

Rubber gloves

Scissors

Spray bottle filled with water

Thermometer

Supplies

1½ teaspoons (10.5 g) Metaphos, if you have hard water

2 teaspoons (5 g) each of 2 MX Fiber-Reactive Dye colors (see "Color Mixing" on pages 41–45)

1½ cups (270 g) noniodized table salt

¼ cup (27 g) PRO Dye Activator

1½ yards (1.46 m) scoured, 100% cotton muslin (see pages 22–24)

½ teaspoon (1.25 ml) Synthrapol (minimum)

Procedure

1. Cover your work table with the plastic drop cloth.
2. Cut the fabric into 6 fat quarters, 18" x 22" (46 cm x 56 cm), or 6 long quarters, 9" x 44" (23 cm x 112 cm). If your scoured fabric is dry, soak it in 1 gallon (4 L) of 110° F (44° C) water with ¼ teaspoon (1.25 g) of Synthrapol for 10 to 15 minutes.
3. Fill 1 bucket half full with warm water. Use this as a rinse bucket to wash your gloved hands between additions to each dye bath.
4. Label the remaining buckets with masking tape. Number them 1–6. Place the buckets in numerical order, from left to right, on your work table. Place a spoon in each bucket.
5. Pour 3 cups (750 ml) of 95° F (35° C) water into each bucket.
6. Add ¼ cup (45 g) of salt to each bucket. Stir until dissolved.
7. If you have hard water, add ¼ teaspoon (1.2 g) of Metaphos to each bucket. Stir until dissolved.
8. Follow the instructions for mixing dye concentrate on pages 48–50. To make the first color, dissolve 2 teaspoons (5 g) of dye powder in 1 cup (250 ml) of 95° F (35° C) water. Repeat this process to make the second color.
9. Fill the 1-quart (1-L) container with 95° F (35° C) water.
10. Measure the dye concentrate for the first color into the buckets as follows:

    Bucket #1: Measure ½ cup (125 ml) of the dye concentrate into the bucket and stir. **1**

    Buckets #2–#5: Using the water from the container you filled in step 9, refill the dye-concentrate cup to the 1-cup (250-ml) mark. Measure ½ cup (125 ml) of the diluted dye concentrate into bucket #2 and stir. Repeat this process for buckets #3, #4, and #5, continuing to dilute the dye concentrate. Do not add this concentrate to bucket #6. Discard the remaining ½ cup (125 ml) of dye concentrate.
11. Measure the dye concentrate for the second color into the buckets as follows:

1

Bucket #6: Measure ½ cup (125 ml) of the dye concentrate into the bucket and stir. **2**

Buckets #5–#2: Using the water from the container you filled in step 9, refill the dye-concentrate cup to the 1-cup (250-ml) mark. Measure ½ cup (125 ml) of the diluted dye concentrate into bucket #5 and stir. Repeat this process for buckets #4, #3, and #2, continuing to dilute the dye concentrate. Do not add this concentrate to bucket #1. Discard the remaining ½ cup (125 ml) of dye concentrate.

12. To make the fixative, dissolve ¼ cup (27 g) of PRO Dye Activator in 1½ cups (375 ml) of 110° to 120°F (44° to 50°C) water; use the 1-quart (1-L) container for mixing.

13. Measure ¼ cup (63 ml) of the fixative into each of the 6 plastic cups. Place one cup in front of each dye bath.

14. Make sure the fabric is completely wet before adding it to the dye baths. If you are not sure that the fabric is completely wet, add ¼ teaspoon (1.25 ml) of Synthrapol to each dye bath before adding the fabric.

15. Add a piece of wet fabric to each dye bath. Set the timer for 15 minutes. Stir the fabric in each dye bath for about 30 seconds, beginning with bucket #1 and ending with bucket #6. Make sure there are no air bubbles trapped in the fabric, and rearrange the folds as you stir. Repeat this process until the timer rings.

   If you use your gloved hands to stir the fabric, make sure to rinse them in the bucket prepared in step 3 before proceeding to the next dye bath.

16. When the timer rings, remove the fabric from bucket #1 and set it aside on a plastic plate. Pour the fixative from the plastic cup into the dye bath and stir. Return the fabric and stir. Repeat this process for all the dye baths, rinsing your gloved hands before proceeding to the next dye bath. **3**

17. Set the timer for 60 minutes. Stir the fabric in each dye bath for about 30 seconds, beginning with bucket #1 and ending with

2

bucket #6. Repeat this process for 15 minutes, then once every 5 minutes until the timer rings.

Stirring at this stage is very important for level dyeing. Make sure to rearrange the folds frequently.

18. When the timer rings, carry each bucket to a sink and remove the fabric. Pour the dye bath down the drain and put the fabric back in the empty bucket.

19. To rinse and wash the fabric by hand, fill each bucket half full with 65° to 75° F (18° to 24° C) water. Swish the fabric around for a minute or so; then pour the rinse water down the drain. Rinse again. Repeat this process for each bucket. After the first 2 rinses, put all the fabric in 1 bucket and repeat the rinse process at least twice. When the fabric feels squeaky clean (not soapy), remove it and empty the rinse bucket. (It's okay for the rinse water to be colored.) Refill the bucket with 140° F (60° C) water. Add ¼ teaspoon (1.25 g) of Synthrapol per yard of fabric. Return the fabric to the rinse bucket and swish it around for 5 minutes. Rinse the fabric in warm (comfortable to the touch) water.

To rinse and wash the fabric by machine, set your washing machine on the small load, warm wash, and warm rinse cycles. Wring out each piece of fabric. After the machine fills and begins to agitate, add the fabric. Distribute it evenly around the tub. Close the lid and let the machine continue through the wash, rinse, and spin cycles. After the final spin cycle, reset the machine on the hot wash and warm rinse cycles. After the machine fills with water, add ¼ teaspoon (1.25 ml) of Synthrapol per yard of fabric and let the machine continue through all the cycles. Check the last rinse cycle. If the rinse water is colored, you may need to repeat this step. For dark colors, 2 short wash treatments may work better than 1 long wash.

20. Dry the fabric in a clothes dryer or on a clothesline. Follow the dryer manufacturer's instructions for the appropriate heat setting.

21. Clean up, using the cellulose sponge, rags, or paper towels.

ADAPTING THE GRADATION RECIPES

The gradation recipes in this book are calibrated for ¼ yard (23 cm) pieces of muslin for each value or hue. If you are like me, you'll want to dye larger and larger pieces of fabric (just to make sure you have enough, of course) or extend the number of steps in the gradations. Use the tables below to adapt the gradation recipes.

Gradation Dyeing Calculations

For each dye bath, use the amounts listed below:

	English	Metric	English	Metric	English	Metric
Fabric	½ yd	46 cm	1 yd	91 cm	2 yd	1.82 m
Metaphos	¼ tsp	1.2 g	⅜ tsp	2.3 g	⅝ tsp	4.5 g
PRO Dye Activator	2½ tsp	7.5 g	5 tsp	15 g	10 tsp	30 g
Salt	4 Tbl	90 g	½ cup	180 g	1¼ cups	360 g
Water	6 cups	1.5 L	3 qt	3 L	1½ gal	6 L

Dye Powder

For a single dye bath, use the amounts listed in the table below. For gradation dyeing, double the amount of dye powder. When dyeing more than 6 steps, double the dark value amount and use 2 cups (500 ml) water to mix the dye concentrate and 1 cup (250 ml) of dye concentrate for each dye bath.

	English	Metric	English	Metric	English	Metric
Fabric	½ yd	46 cm	1 yd	91 cm	2 yd	1.82 m
Dye powder for:						
Light value	¼ tsp	0.38 g	⅜ tsp	0.75 g	⅝ tsp	1.5 g
Medium value	⅞ tsp	2.4 g	1¾ tsp	4.5 g	3⅝ tsp	9 g
Dark value*	1¾ tsp	4.5 g	3⅝ tsp	9 g	7¼ tsp	18 g

For black, double the amount of dye powder and extend the dyeing time to 90 minutes (after adding activator).

CREATING PATTERNS WITH RESISTS

A "resist" is anything that prevents dye from penetrating a fabric—creating a pattern based on the undyed and dyed areas. You can create resist patterns by manipulating the fabric, as described in this section, or by using a liquid resist (see pages 120–25). This section describes different ways to fold, pleat, roll, clamp, knot, bunch, bind, and stitch (including overstitching, gathering, pleating, and complex machine stitching) to produce a desired pattern.

Creating patterns with resists is an art form. The photos in this section show just a few patterns you can experiment with in your immersion dye baths; I encourage you to be adventurous. For more ideas, see pages 102–5. Following are some guidelines:

- Bundled fabric takes up less space and uses less water than other immersion dye bath methods. You can decrease the amount of water and salt (in proportion) in the dye bath if desired; just make sure the fabric is completely submerged. Using less water (with the same amount of dye powder) produces darker colors. Keep notes on the changes you make to the dye bath.
- Create complex patterns by overdyeing different colors and patterns. For example, fold a piece of fabric and dye it light blue, then unfold and fold in another direction and dye the fabric yellow. The resulting fabric will have patterned areas that are white, yellow, blue, and various shades of green.

Twisting and Coiling

Twist fabric lengthwise as shown. Hold the two ends together, allowing the fabric to twist together as shown. Wrap a rubber band around the ends.

Twisted and Coiled Fabric

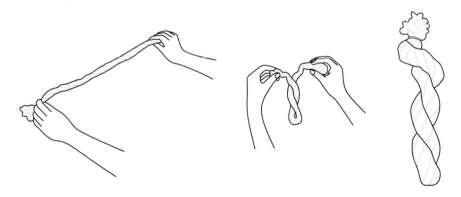

Clamping

Fold the fabric into an accordion shape, alternating folds, then fold the accordion in one direction as shown. Use a clamp to hold the shape during immersion dyeing.

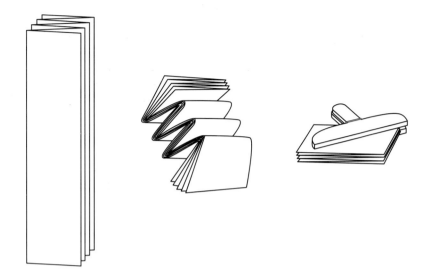

Clamped Fabric

Pole Wrapping

Purchase a segment of polyvinyl chloride (PVC) pipe. To make a sleeve, cut a piece of fabric slightly larger than the pipe, then stitch the long edges as shown. Place the sleeve on the pipe. Twist the sleeve around the pipe, pushing it down ("ruching") as you work. The tighter the ruching, the crisper the pattern. Use masking tape or large rubber bands to hold the ruching during immersion dyeing.

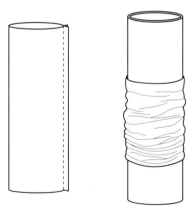

Pole-Wrapped Fabric

Stitching

Running Stitch: Use a double length of heavy thread, such as button-and-carpet thread. Sew lines of running stitches across the fabric, varying the stitch length if desired. Pull the threads very tight as shown, then knot the doubled ends.

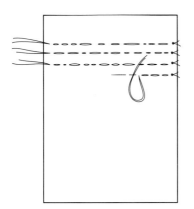 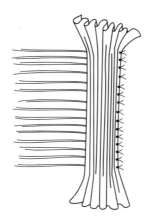

Fabrics Prepared with a Running Stitch

Whipstitch: Use a double length of heavy thread, such as button-and-carpet thread. Fold your fabric, then whipstitch the folded edge, varying the stitch depth and length if desired. Pull the threads tight as shown, then knot the doubled ends.

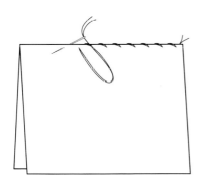 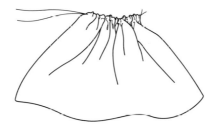

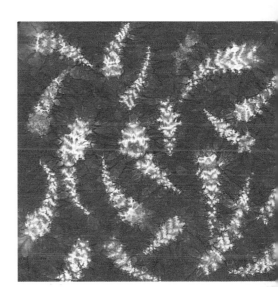

Whipstitched Fabric

Helpful Hint

Removing Stitching

Let fabric dry before removing thread. Grasp the dyed, dry bundle in one hand and pull the thread ends with the other. Slip a seam ripper under the knot and cut it off. Cut all the knots off before opening the fabric to prevent cutting the fabric by mistake.

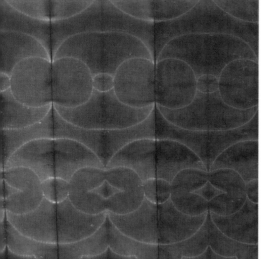

Katano-Stitched Fabric

Katano stitch: Fold the fabric into an accordion shape. Press. Machine or hand stitch (with a running stitch) as shown.

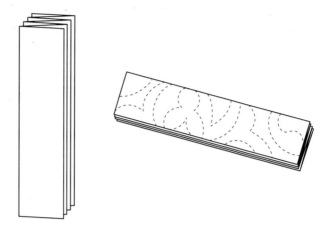

Fold-and-Edge Stitched Fabric

Fold and Edge Stitch: Use a double length of heavy thread, such as button-and-carpet thread. Make a small pleat in your fabric. Using a running stitch, sew the pleat in place. Repeat as many times as desired. Pull the threads tight as shown, then knot the doubled ends.

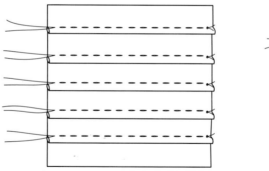

Tucked and Stitched Fabric, Both Sides

Tuck and Stitch: Make even vertical pleats every few inches, machine basting as shown. Then make even horizontal pleats every few inches, machine basting each pleat.

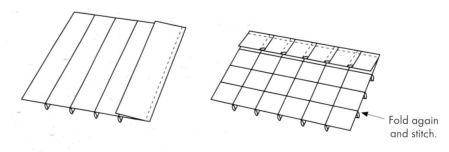

Fold again and stitch.

TROUBLESHOOTING

The color is not as bright as it should be. There are six possible causes. There may not have been enough dye in the dye bath, the water may have been too hot or cold, the water used to dissolve the dye may have been too hot, there may be a finish on the fabric, the fabric may not be 100% cotton, and/or the dye may be too old. **1**

You may have to work through a process of elimination. Use more dye powder, check the temperature of the water (both the dye concentrate and dye bath), do the water-drop test (see page 24), scour the fabric again, use different fabric, or purchase new dye.

The dye washes off in the rinse water. There are three possible causes. There may be a finish on the fabric, the water used to dissolve the dye may have been too hot, and/or you may have forgotten to add the fixative. **2**

Again, work through a process of elimination. Do the water-drop test (see page 24), check the temperature of the water, scour the fabric again, and/or use different fabric.

There are round and spotty cloud-like shapes on the dyed fabric. Either there is a finish or other additive on the fabric (Did you wash or scour the fabric with a commercial detergent containing brightener or softener?), or air bubbles were trapped in the fabric during the dye cycle. Scour the fabric again, referring to the recipe on pages 22–24, or use a different fabric. During dyeing, make sure you squeeze all the air bubbles out of the fabric. **3**

There are icicle-like shapes on the dyed fabric. Folds in the fabric acted as a resist, preventing level dyeing. Stir! Stir! Stir! Start again with undyed fabric and stir more often, making sure to rearrange the folds frequently. **4**

There are pindots of concentrated color on the dyed fabric. The dye was not fully dissolved. Use more water to dissolve the dye powder and strain the dye concentrate through several layers of nylon stocking or cheesecloth before adding it to the dye bath, or add one teaspoon (4 g) to one tablespoon (12 g) of urea to the dye concentrate. Some dyes (particularly yellows, reds, and blacks) dissolve more slowly than others. The urea increases the solubility of the dye, helping the dye dissolve.

Helpful Hint

Disappointing Fabrics

Fabrics with spots, icicles, clouds, and other problems, as well as fabrics patterned with a resist technique, are great for overdyeing or overprinting with dyes or pigments!

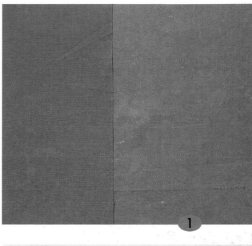

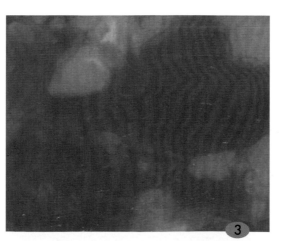

⌃ *Sleepless*
by Linda Levin, 1995, Wayland, Massachusetts, 69" x 52". **Method**: Fiber-reactive dye on cotton. Machine pieced and quilted. Photo by Joe Ofria at The Image Inn.

❯ *Composition III*
by Linda Levin, 1993, Wayland, Massachusetts, 30" x 40". **Method**: Fiber-reactive dye on cotton. Machine pieced and quilted. Photo by Joe Ofria at The Image Inn.

< *Pikadon: Hiroshima Series* by Barbara Moll, 1996, Muncie, Indiana, 41" x 64". **Method:** Whole-cloth quilt. Fiber-reactive dye on cotton. Hand painted. Machine quilted with laminated fabric details. Photo by Joan Whitaker

∨ *Pallone: Lowtano da Siena* by Linda Levin, 1987, Wayland, Massachusetts, 53" x 49". **Method:** Fiber-reactive dye on cotton. Machine pieced and quilted. Photo by Joe Ofria at The Image Inn.

> *Flow*
by Natasha Kempers-Cullen, 1992, Topsham, Maine,
85" x 69". **Method**: Whole-cloth quilt. Fiber-reactive
dye and textile paint on cotton. Hand painted and
stamped. Machine pieced and machine and hand
quilted. Hand embroidered and embellished with glass
beads, fetishes, and shells. Photo by Dennis Griggs.

< *Mira, the Wonderful Star*
by Diana Dabinett, 1995, Torbay, Newfoundland,
Canada, 40" x 67½". **Method**: Fiber-reactive dye on
silk. Hand painted using resist. Photo by the artist.

V *Atrium*
by Elizabeth Owen, 1994, Baton Rouge, Louisiana,
60" x 71". **Method**: Fiber-reactive dye on cotton.
Machine pieced and hand embroidered and quilted.
Photo by Ron E. Dobbs.

⌐ *Bear at Crossroads*
by Mia Rozmyn, 1996, Seattle, Washington, 44" x 33".
Method: Hand-dyed silk. Machine pieced and quilted.
Photo by the artist.

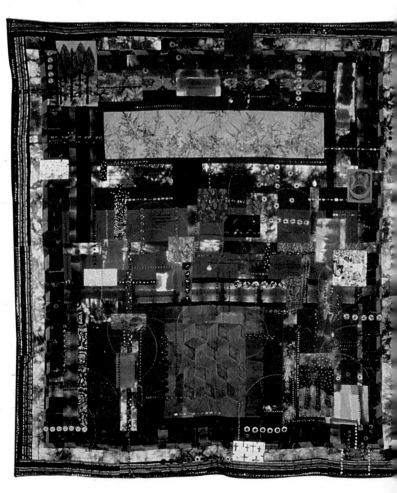

▲ *Sweet Aquarian*
by Kathleen O'Connor, 1997, Putney,
Vermont, 75" x 47". **Method**: Fiber-
reactive dye and textile paint on cotton.
Machine pieced and quilted. Photo by
Mark Corliss.

❯ *Mountain Aspens*
by Lenore Davis, 1994, Newport,
Kentucky, 60" x 60". This is the last quilt
Lenore made before her untimely death in
1995. **Method**: Whole-cloth quilt. Fiber-
reactive dye and textile paint on cotton
velveteen. Monoprinted. Hand quilted.

∧ Sails
by Mickey Lawler, 1992, West Hartford, Connecticut, 58" x 47". **Method**: Textile paint on cotton. Hand painted. Machine pieced and hand quilted. Photo by Jack McConnell.

< Faces II
by Elizabeth Hendricks, 1995, Seattle, Washington, 40" x 54". **Method**: Hand-dyed and commercially dyed fabrics. Machine pieced and quilted. Photo by Roger Schreiber.

Direct-Application Dye Techniques

Using direct-application techniques, you can create fabric with many different colors (including all three primary colors). There are many distinctive and inspirational direct-application techniques; this section covers fold-and-dip dyeing, tie dyeing, color washing, hand painting, monoprinting, and stamping. Also included are silk-painting techniques for cotton fabric and using a prepared resist.

For all these techniques, you apply a concentrated dye-stock solution and auxiliary products to the fabric. This concentrated solution can be thick (like jelly), thin (like water), or any consistency in between. After the dye is applied, the fabric is left to cure for a specific amount of time. The excess dye is rinsed and washed out, then the fabric is dried.

There are many ways to fix dye when using a direct-application technique. This book focuses on the two most popular methods: activator soak and mixed alkali. Each direct-application recipe includes a fixing-method recommendation based on my experiences with dye fixing prematurely, ease of washout, and length of time needed to create a pattern. I encourage you to try both methods. See "Activator Soak and Mixed Alkali" on pages 60–63 for guidelines.

Treat yourself to mercerized cotton for your first attempts. Your time and energy will be rewarded with fabric that is rich in color and visual texture. Review "Protecting Yourself and Your Environment" on pages 16–17 for guidelines on working with dye and auxiliary powders.

FOLD-AND-DIP DYE

For fold-and-dip dyeing, you fold fabric into an accordion shape, then dip it in dye-stock solution. The resulting fabric has a delicate geometric pattern; the size of the folds and the fabric weight determine the pattern scale. The thinner the fabric, the easier it is to fold and the more manageable. It is difficult to dye large pieces and heavy-weight fabrics, but not impossible. You do not need to dye the entire bundle; some areas can be left white as part of the design.

Use this recipe to fold-and-dip dye 2 to 3 yards (1.82 to 2.74 m) of 100% cotton muslin. I recommend adding mixed alkali to the dye-stock solution. Mark the time on the container of dye-stock solution; you have 4 hours to use it.

Read through the directions and assemble all the necessary equipment and supplies before you begin. Wear a dust/mist mask or respirator while working with dye powder and auxiliary products, and remember to wear rubber gloves when you work with the fabric and liquid dye.

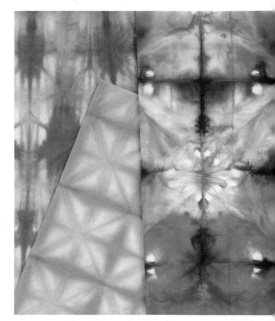

Fold-and-Dip Dyed Fabrics

Equipment

Two 2-gallon (8-L) plastic buckets (1 bucket is optional)

Cellulose sponge, rags, or paper towels

Clothesline and clothespins (optional)

Measuring cups and spoons or scale

Mixing box (see page 35)

Newspapers

Plastic drop cloth

Plastic or Styrofoam plates

Rubber gloves

Stirring tools

Thermometer

Watch or clock

Wide-mouth plastic containers (one for each color you want to use)

Supplies

2 to 3 yards (1.82 to 2.74 m) scoured, 100% cotton muslin
(see pages 22–24)*

½ cup (125 ml) each of at least 3 colors of dye-stock solution
(see pages 50–52)

½ teaspooon (2 g) mixed alkali per ½ cup (125 ml) of dye-stock solution
(see pages 62–63)

¼ teaspoon (1.25 ml) Synthrapol (minimum)

*Begin with small pieces of fabric, ¼ yard (23 cm) or smaller. As you become comfort-able with fold-and-dip dyeing, increase the size of your pieces.

98

Procedure

1. Cover your work table with the plastic drop cloth.
2. Fill a bucket half full with warm (comfortable to the touch) water. Use this as a rinse bucket for washing your gloved hands.
3. Accordion-fold the fabric into a narrow strip. Fold again into a triangle or square, repeating to complete an accordion fold as shown. For sharp folds, press the fabric before dyeing.

Fold into accordion triangle:

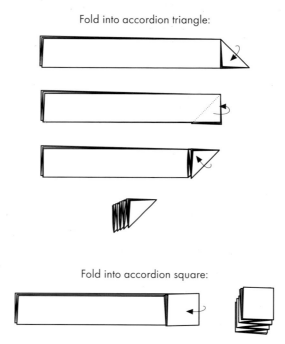

Fold into accordion square:

4. Prepare ½ cup (125 ml) dye-stock solution for each color you want to use. When the dye is completely dissolved, pour each solution into a wide-mouth container.
5. Prepare the mixed alkali: add ½ teaspoon (2 g) of the mixed alkali powder to each ½ cup (125 ml) of dye-stock solution. Stir until the powder dissolves. Note the time; discard the dye-stock solution after 4 hours.
6. Dip a corner of the folded fabric into one of the dye-stock solutions. Squeeze excess solution back into the container. Turn the fabric and dip another corner into a different color. Repeat this process for the third and fourth corners. Place the fabric on a plastic or Styrofoam plate and check the folds to be sure the fabric is completely saturated. **1 2 3**
7. Allow the fabric to cure at a temperature **above 70° F (21° C)** for a minimum of 24 hours. See page 62 for ways to maintain the curing temperature.
8. After curing, rinse and wash the fabric by hand or machine. To rinse and wash by hand, fill a bucket half full with 65° to 75° F (18° to 24° C) water. Carefully unfold the fabric and open it completely. **4**

Carefully and quickly immerse the fabric in the bucket of rinse water. It is important to keep the fabric moving during the entire rinse process so that the dye colors do not stain another part of the fabric. Swish the fabric around the bucket for 1 to 2 minutes. Remove the fabric and change the rinse water. Repeat this rinse 3 to 4 times. You may want to use 2 rinse buckets; the second bucket will be ready and waiting when it is time to change water. When the fabric feels squeaky clean (not soapy), remove it and empty the rinse bucket. (It's okay if you still see color in the rinse water, so long as the fabric feels squeaky clean.) Refill the bucket with 140° F (60° C) water. Add ¼ teaspoon (1.25 ml) of Synthrapol per yard of fabric. Return the fabric to the bucket and swish it around for 5 minutes. Rinse the fabric in warm (comfortable to the touch) water.

To rinse and wash the fabric by machine, set your washing machine on the small load, warm wash, and warm rinse cycles. After the machine fills and begins to agitate, carefully unfold the fabric and open it completely. Add the fabric, distributing it evenly around the tub. Close the lid and let the machine continue through the wash, rinse, and spin cycles. After the final spin cycle, reset the machine on the hot wash and warm rinse cycles. After the machine fills with water, add ¼ teaspoon (1.25 ml) of Synthrapol per yard of fabric and let the machine continue through all the cycles. Check the last rinse cycle. If the rinse water is colored, you may need to repeat this step. For dark colors, 2 short wash treatments may work better than 1 long wash.

9. Dry the fabric in a clothes dryer or on a clothesline. Follow the dryer manufacturer's instructions for the appropriate heat setting.

10. Clean up, using the cellulose sponge, rags, or paper towels.

TIE DYE

Tie dye is a technique that can produce simple or sophisticated patterns. Use this easy recipe to tie-dye 2 to 3 yards (1.82 to 2.74 m) of 100% cotton muslin.

I recommend that you prepare the fabric in activator soak, fold as described on pages 102–5, then apply the dye-stock solution while the fabric is still wet or damp. Experiment by soaking fabric in the activator and drying it before dyeing. Keep notes on your experiments so you can repeat those "happy accidents."

Read through the directions and assemble all the necessary equipment and supplies before you begin. Wear a dust/mist mask or respirator while working with dye powder and auxiliary products, and remember to wear rubber gloves when you work with the fabric and liquid dye.

Experimenting with Fold-and-Dip Dyeing

Try dampening the fabric bundle before dyeing. Dampening the fabric decreases its absorbency, and the resulting color is lighter. Or, for lighter values, dilute the dye-stock solution with activated urea water.

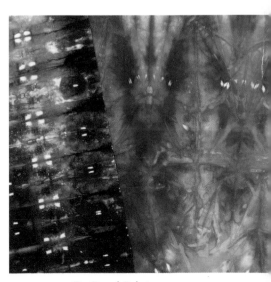

Tie-Dyed Fabrics

Equipment

Two 2-gallon (8-L) plastic buckets (1 bucket is optional)

Cellulose sponge, rags, or paper towels

Clothesline and clothespins (optional)

Funnel (optional)

Kitchen timer or watch

Measuring cups and spoons or scale

Plastic drop cloth

Plastic or Styrofoam plates

Rubber bands, string, or clothespins

Rubber gloves

Scissors

Sponge brushes and/or syringes (optional)

Squeeze bottles (1 bottle for each dye-stock solution and additional bottles if you want to mix colors)

Stirring tools

Thermometer

Supplies

2 to 3 yards (1.82 to 2.74 m) scoured, 100% cotton muslin*
(see pages 22–24)

1 gallon (4 L) activator soak (see pages 60–62)

½ cup (125 ml) each of at least 4 colors of dye-stock solution
(see pages 50–52)

¼ teaspoon (1.25 ml) Synthrapol (minimum)

Urea water (optional)

*Begin with small pieces of fabric, ¼ yard (23 cm) or smaller. As you become comfortable with tie dyeing, increase the size of your pieces.

Procedure

1. Cover your work table with the plastic drop cloth.
2. Fill a plastic bucket half full with warm (comfortable to the touch) water. Use this as a rinse bucket for your gloved hands.
3. Prepare the activator soak. Place the scoured fabric in the activator soak and set the timer for 15 minutes. Stir periodically. Make sure the fabric is completely submerged and can move freely.
4. When the timer rings, remove the fabric and wring it out. **Do not rinse!** Fold the fabric into the shape you want and secure it with rubber bands, string, or clothespins (see pages 102–5).
5. Prepare ½ cup (125 ml) of dye-stock solution for each color you want to use. When the dye is completely dissolved, pour each solution into a squeeze bottle. (You may want to use a funnel.)

6. Place the folded, damp fabric on a plastic or Styrofoam plate. Apply the dye-stock solution to the fabric with squeeze bottles, sponge brushes, or syringes. Check the folds of the fabric to make sure the dye has soaked through. Avoid overlaying more than 2 colors. Overlaying 3 primary colors produces brown. **1** **2**

    Gently massage the fabric between your gloved fingers to ensure that the colors blend. Carefully turn the fabric over and apply the dye to the other side.

    Take care not to apply so much dye that it runs into a pool on the plate. If this happens, gently squeeze out the excess dye and carefully move the dyed fabric to a clean plate. **3**

    For lighter values, dilute the dye-stock solution with activated urea water.

    Don't be alarmed by the murky black appearance of your fabric; the rinse and wash process will remove any unfixed dye. The finished colors will be clear and several shades lighter.

7. Allow the fabric to cure at a temperature **above 70° F (21° C)** for a minimum of 4 hours. For dark colors and turquoise, allow the fabric to cure for a minimum of 24 hours. See page 62 for ways to maintain the curing temperature.

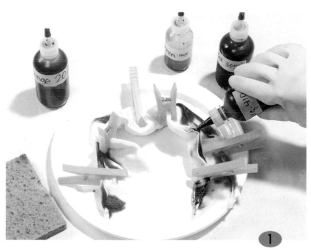

8. After curing, rinse and wash the fabric by hand or machine. To rinse and wash by hand, fill a bucket half full with 65° to 75° F (18° to 24° C) water. Carefully unfold the fabric and open it completely. Carefully and quickly immerse the fabric in the bucket of rinse water. It is important to keep the fabric moving during the entire rinse process so that the dye colors do not stain another part of the fabric. Swish the fabric around the bucket for 1 to 2 minutes. Remove the fabric and change the rinse water. Repeat this rinse 3 to 4 times. You may want to use 2 rinse buckets; the second bucket will be ready and waiting when it is time to change water. **4**

When the fabric feels squeaky clean (not soapy), remove it and empty the rinse bucket. (It's okay if you still see color in the rinse water, so long as the fabric feels squeaky clean.) Refill the bucket with 140° F (60° C) water. Add ¼ teaspoon (1.25 ml) of Synthrapol per yard of fabric. Return the fabric to the bucket and swish it around for 5 minutes. Rinse the fabric in warm (comfortable to the touch) water.

To rinse and wash the fabric by machine, set your washing machine on the small load, warm wash, and warm rinse cycles. After the machine fills and begins to agitate, carefully unfold the fabric and open it completely. Add the fabric, distributing it evenly around the tub. Close the lid and let the machine continue through the wash, rinse, and spin cycles. After the final spin cycle, reset the machine on the hot wash and warm rinse cycles. After the machine fills with water, add ¼ teaspoon (1.25 ml) of Synthrapol per yard of fabric and let the machine continue through all the cycles. Check the last rinse cycle. If the rinse water is colored, you may need to repeat this step. For dark colors, 2 short wash treatments may work better than 1 long wash.

9. Dry the fabric in a clothes dryer or on a clothesline. Follow the dryer manufacturer's instructions for the appropriate heat setting.

10. Clean up, using the cellulose sponge, rags, or paper towels.

CREATING PATTERNS WITH RESISTS

As explained on page 85, you can fold, pleat, roll, clamp, knot, bunch, bind, and/or stitch your fabric, working neatly or loosely, to produce original and elegant visual textures. The following are more examples showing the range of pattern you can create. Remember, there are no wrong ways to fold, bind, or tie your fabric, only variations! Experiment to find your favorites.

Lumpy Pancake

Working with your gloved fingertips, pinch wet fabric into a lumpy pancake. Place the fabric pancake on a leak-proof tray or plate before applying dye-stock solution.

Lumpy-Pancake Fabrics

Accordion

Fold the fabric into an accordion shape. Use clothespins or bull-dog clips to hold the shape.

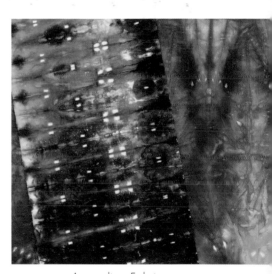

Accordion Fabrics

Bias Accordion

Working on the bias, fold the fabric into an accordion shape. Use clothespins or bulldog clips to hold the shape.

Bias-Accordion Fabrics

Double-Chevron Fabric

Double Chevron

Fold the fabric into an accordion shape. Press the folds. Fold again on the bias (diagonally).

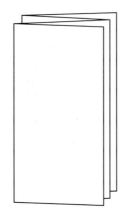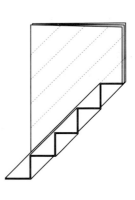

Uneven-Accordion-Fold
and-Zigzag-Stitched Fabric

Uneven Accordion Fold and Zigzag Stitch

Fold the fabric into an uneven accordion shape. Using a machine zigzag stitch, stitch each fold.

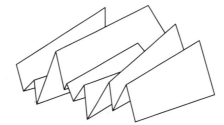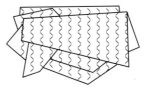

Accordion-Circle Fabric

Accordion Circle

Fold the fabric in half, then make triangle-shaped accordion folds from the center. Use rubber bands or string to hold the shape.

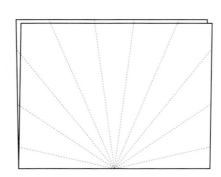

Spiral-Folded Chevron

Fold the fabric into an accordion shape. Press the folds. Fold triangles, working back and forth as shown. Use clothespins to hold the triangles.

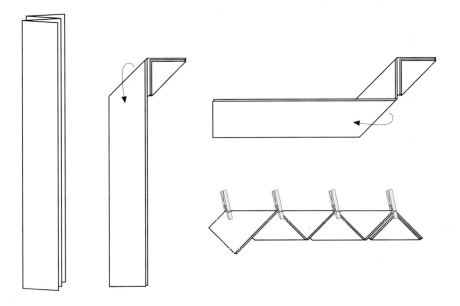

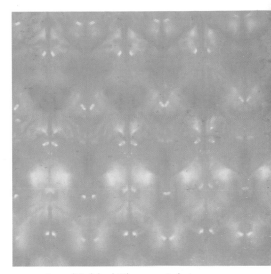

Spiral-Folded-Chevron Fabric

Machine Zigzag Stitch

Fold the fabric into knife pleats and press the folds. Using a machine zigzag stitch, sew each pleat in place.

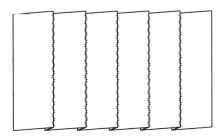

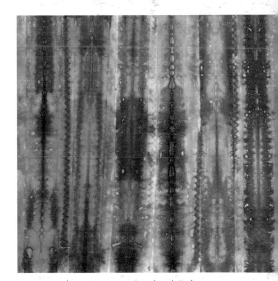

Machine-Zigzag-Stitched Fabric

Color-Wash Fabric

HAND PAINTING A COLOR WASH

A color wash can transition gently from one value or color to another or blend in complex layers. As you paint, move your arm from the elbow rather than just moving your hand at the wrist. Practice will give your work a looseness and fluency.

This recipe is for painting a hue gradation using thin dye paste. I recommend that you prepare the fabric with activator soak as described below, then apply thin dye paste to wet or damp fabric. (It is easier to blend and create subtle shading on damp or wet fabric.)

Use this recipe to hand paint 1 to 2 yards (91 cm to 1.82 m) of 100% cotton muslin. Read through the directions and assemble all the necessary equipment and supplies before you begin. Wear a dust/mist mask or respirator while working with dye powder and auxiliary products, and remember to wear rubber gloves when you work with the fabric and liquid dye.

Equipment

2-gallon (8-L) plastic bucket (optional)

Artists' stretcher frame or embroidery hoop
(or pin the fabric between 2 sawhorses)

Assortment of wide-mouth containers with lids (one for each color you want to use and one for rinsing the brushes)

Cellulose sponge, rags, or paper towels

Clothesline and clothespins (optional)

Masking tape or T-pins

Measuring cups and spoons or scale

Plastic drop cloth

Rubber gloves

Sponge brushes, ½" to 2½" (1.27 cm to 6.3 cm) wide

Stirring tools

Thermometer

Watch or clock

Supplies

1 to 2 yards (91 cm to 1.82 m) scoured, 100% cotton muslin
(see pages 22–23)*

1 gallon (4 L) activator soak (see pages 60–62)

½ cup (125 ml) each of at least 2 colors of thin dye paste (see pages 58–60)

¼ teaspoon (1.25 ml) Synthrapol (minimum)

Activated print paste (optional)

Activated urea water (optional)

*Begin with small pieces of fabric, ¼ yard (23 cm) or smaller. As you become comfortable with hand painting, increase the size of your pieces.

Procedure

1. Cover your work table with the plastic drop cloth.
2. Stretch the fabric on the artists' stretcher frame or embroidery hoop and secure it with masking tape or T-pins.
3. Fill a wide-mouth container half full with warm (comfortable to the touch) water. Use this to rinse your brushes between colors, or use different brushes for each color. This helps ensure a clean transition between colors or values.
4. Prepare the activator soak. Using a sponge brush, apply the activator soak to the fabric. Make sure the fabric is completely wet. Re-pin the fabric so it is held taut. If the fabric sags during the painting process, the dye will migrate to the sagging area, making it darker. **1**
5. Prepare ½ cup (125 ml) of thin dye paste for each color you want to use. Pour each color of thin dye paste into a wide-mouth container.
6. Using a clean sponge brush and long, even horizontal strokes, apply one color of thin dye paste to the bottom third of the fabric (from the bottom edge). Using a clean sponge brush, apply the second color to the upper third of the fabric (from the top edge). Apply only a small amount of color with each stroke; it is much easier to add color than to remove it!

   Blend the colors together in the middle, blending the edges of each stroke for the smoothest transition. **2**
7. Allow the fabric to cure at a temperature **above 70° F (21° C)** for a minimum of 4 hours. For dark colors and turquoise, allow the fabric to cure for a minimum of 24 hours. See page 62 for ways to maintain the curing temperature. If the fabric appears to be drying out, cover it with plastic wrap.

Experimenting with a Color Wash

Try one of the following.

- Paint very wet, just damp, and dry fabric. Each produces different results. The wetter the fabric, the more migration of color and the lighter the final color. It's easier to blend colors on wet fabric.

- Allow the fabric to dry slightly after you paint it. Remove it from your work table and hang it from a clothesline so the dye will migrate. Place newspaper underneath the damp fabric to catch drips.

- Use T-pins to secure lengths of fabric between two sawhorses. When the fabric gets wet and stretches, there will be no need to unpin. Just move the sawhorses to take the sag out of the fabric.

Hand-Painted Fabric

8. After curing, rinse and wash the fabric by hand or machine. To rinse and wash by hand, fill the bucket half full with 65° to 75° F (18° to 24° C) water. Carefully remove the fabric from the artists' stretcher frame or embroidery hoop. Immerse the fabric in the bucket of rinse water. It is important to keep the fabric moving during the entire rinse process so that the dye colors do not stain another part of the fabric. Swish the fabric around the bucket for 1 to 2 minutes. Remove the fabric and change the rinse water. Repeat this rinse 3 to 4 times. You may want to use 2 rinse buckets; the second bucket will be ready and waiting when it is time to change water. When the fabric feels squeaky clean (not soapy), remove it and empty the rinse bucket. (It's okay if you still see color in the rinse water, so long as the fabric feels squeaky clean.) Refill the bucket with 140° F (60° C) water. Add ¼ teaspoon (1.25 ml) of Synthrapol per yard of fabric. Return the fabric to the bucket and swish it around for 5 minutes. Rinse the fabric in warm (comfortable to the touch) water.

   To rinse and wash the fabric by machine, set your washing machine on the small load, warm wash, and warm rinse cycles. After the machine fills and begins to agitate, carefully remove the fabric from the artists' stretcher frame or embroidery hoop and add it to the machine. Close the lid and let the machine continue through the wash, rinse, and spin cycles. After the final spin cycle, reset the machine on the hot wash and warm rinse cycles. After the machine fills with water, add ¼ teaspoon (1.25 ml) of Synthrapol per yard of fabric and let the machine continue through all the cycles. Check the last rinse cycle. If the rinse water is colored, you may need to repeat this step. For dark colors, 2 short wash treatments may work better than 1 long wash.

9. Dry the fabric in a clothes dryer or on a clothesline. Follow the dryer manufacturer's instructions for the appropriate heat setting.

10. Clean up, using the cellulose sponge, rags, or paper towels.

HAND PAINTING A DESIGN

Hand painting is a versatile technique and easier than you may think. Draw or transfer a design to fabric using a soft pencil, then fill in the design with thin or thick dye paste. Fabric responds well to traditional watercolor techniques such as watermarks, dry brush, wet on wet, and dry on dry.

You can apply thick dye paste with a sponge brush, artists' brush, syringe, or squeeze bottle. Your brush strokes can be bold, loose, or tightly controlled. Using a 12" x 12" (30 cm x 30 cm) square of muslin, experiment with brushes to see how many different marks you can make. Pull, push, twist, roll, and dab the brushes to create interesting textures and patterns. ❶ Note: these marks will look different on different-weight and -weave fabrics.

Use this recipe to paint 1 to 2 yards (91 cm to 1.82 m) of 100% cotton muslin. I recommend adding mixed alkali to the thin dye paste. You can paint up to 3 colors on top of one another; additional colors will probably not be able to penetrate to the fabric. For lighter values, dilute the thin dye paste with activated print paste.

Read through the directions and assemble all the necessary equipment and supplies before you begin. Wear a dust/mist mask or respirator while working with dye powder and auxiliary products, and remember to wear rubber gloves when you work with the fabric and liquid dye.

Equipment

2-gallon (8-L) plastic bucket (optional)

Artists' stretcher frame, embroidery hoop, or canvas-covered padded table

Assortment of artists' brushes, sponge brushes, and syringes

Assortment of wide-mouth plastic containers

Cellulose sponge, rags, or paper towels

Clothesline and clothespins (optional)

Masking tape or T-pins

Measuring cups and spoons or scale

Mixing box (see page 35)

Newspapers

Plastic drop cloth

Rubber gloves

Soft drawing pencil (5b)

Stirring tools

Thermometer

Watch or clock

Supplies

1 to 2 yards (91 cm to 1.82 m) scoured, 100% cotton muslin (see pages 22–24)*

½ cup (125 ml) each of at least 3 colors of thin dye paste (see pages 58–60)

½ tsp (2 g) mixed alkali per ½ cup (125 ml) of thin dye paste (see pages 62–63)

¼ tsp (1.25 ml) Synthrapol (minimum)

Activated print paste (optional)

Activated urea water (optional)

*Begin with small pieces of fabric, ¼ yard (23 cm) or smaller. As you become comfortable with hand painting, increase the size of your pieces.

Making a Light Table at Home

Helpful Hint

Creating Dark Patterns

If you plan to hand paint a pattern with very little white or light area, prepare the fabric in activator soak, allow the fabric to dry before using, and add mixed alkali to the dye-stock solution or dye paste.

Procedure

1. Cover your work table with the plastic drop cloth.

2. Using the soft pencil, draw or transfer a design to your fabric. You may want to make a light table to help you transfer the design. Lay a piece of glass or translucent plastic between 2 tables (or on a table with the leaf removed) and place a lamp underneath.

   You can also use a window or sliding glass door. Tape the pattern to the glass surface; then center the fabric over the pattern. Pull the fabric taut—not taut enough to stretch the fabric—and tape it to the glass.

3. Stretch the fabric on an artists' stretcher frame or embroidery hoop and secure it with masking tape or T-pins, or secure the fabric to a canvas-covered padded table.

4. Fill a wide-mouth container half full with warm (comfortable to the touch) water. Use this to rinse your brushes.

5. Prepare ½ cup (125 ml) thin dye paste for each color you want to use. Pour ½ cup of each color of thin dye paste into a wide-mouth container.

6. Prepare the mixed alkali. Add ½ teaspoon (2 g) of the mixed alkali powder to each ½ cup (125 ml) of thin dye paste. Stir until the powder dissolves. Note the time; discard the dye paste after 4 hours.

7. Apply the dye pastes with artists' brushes, sponge brushes, syringes, or squeeze bottles. Continue painting until the design is complete. Remember, dye paste prepared with mixed alkali is only good for 4 hours. **2**

8. Allow the fabric to cure at a temperature **above 70° F (21° C)** for a minimum of 24 hours. See page 62 for ways to maintain the curing temperature.

9. After curing, rinse and wash the fabric by hand or machine. To rinse and wash by hand, fill the plastic bucket half full with 65° to 75° F (18° to 24° C) water. Carefully remove the fabric from the

artists' stretcher, embroidery hoop, or canvas. Immerse the fabric in the bucket of rinse water. It is important to keep the fabric moving during the entire rinse process so that the dye colors do not stain another part of the fabric. Swish the fabric around the bucket for 1 to 2 minutes. Remove the fabric and change the rinse water. Repeat this rinse 3 to 4 times. You may want to use 2 rinse buckets; the second bucket will be ready and waiting when it is time to change water. When the fabric feels squeaky clean (not soapy), remove it and empty the rinse bucket. (It's okay if you still see color in the rinse water, so long as the fabric feels squeaky clean.) Refill the bucket with 140° F (60° C) water. Add ¼ teaspoon (1.25 ml) of Synthrapol per yard of fabric. Return the fabric to the bucket and swish it around for 5 minutes. Rinse the fabric in warm (comfortable to the touch) water.

To rinse and wash the fabric by machine, set your washing machine on the small load, warm wash, and warm rinse cycles. After the machine fills and begins to agitate, carefully remove the fabric from the artists' stretcher, embroidery hoop, or tabletop and add it to the machine. Close the lid and let the machine continue through the wash, rinse, and spin cycles. After the final spin cycle, reset the machine on the hot wash and warm rinse cycles. After the machine fills with water, add ¼ teaspoon (1.25 ml) of Synthrapol per yard of fabric and let the machine continue through all the cycles. Check the last rinse cycle. If the rinse water is colored, you may need to repeat this step. For dark colors, 2 short wash treatments may work better than 1 long wash.

10. Dry the fabric in a clothes dryer or on a clothesline. Follow the dryer manufacturer's instructions for the appropriate heat setting.

11. Clean up, using the cellulose sponge, rags, or paper towels.

MONOPRINTING

Monoprinting is a transfer printing process that literally means "one print." You begin by painting a design, using your fingers or artist's brushes, on a printing plate: a hard, nonporous surface such as glass, Formica, or clear acrylic. Different surfaces produce different textures. I like to use clear acrylic, lightly brushed with steel wool or fine sandpaper. This surface has enough "tooth" to hold a smooth layer of dye paste.

Use this recipe to print 2 yards (1.82 m) of 100% cotton muslin. I recommend adding mixed alkali to the dye paste. Remember to take notes on the sequence of dye colors. The process can be difficult to reinvent.

Read through the directions and assemble all the necessary equipment and supplies before you begin. Wear a dust/mist mask or respirator while working with dye powder and auxiliary products, and remember to wear rubber gloves when you work with the fabric and liquid dye.

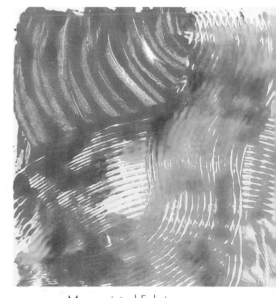

Monoprinted Fabric

Helpful Hint

Monoprinting Tips

I like to use one, or occasionally two, colors for a print. Limiting colors helps prevent your print from becoming muddy.

Put the lightest colors down first, building to the darkest. Do not layer more than three colors.

You need to paint quickly in warm, dry weather. The dye paste doesn't take long to dry.

If you don't like your design, simply wipe it off and start again. When you're satisfied with the design, transfer it to fabric.

Equipment

1 square, 12" x 12" (30 cm x 30 cm), of clear acrylic, lightly brushed with steel wool or sanded on one side
2-gallon (8-L) plastic bucket (optional)
Assortment of artists' brushes, sponge brushes and/or rollers, and syringes
Assortment of wide-mouth plastic containers with lids (one for each color you want to use and one for rinsing the brushes)
Canvas drop cloth
Cellulose sponge, rags, or paper towels
Clothesline and clothespins (optional)
Masking tape or T-pins
Measuring cups and spoons or scale
Mixing box (see page 35)
Newspapers
Padded table
Rubber gloves
Stirring tools
Thermometer
Watch or clock

Supplies

2 yards (1.82 m) scoured, 100% cotton muslin (see pages 22–24)*
½ cup (125 ml) each of 3 or more colors of thick dye paste (see pages 58–60)
½ tsp (2 g) mixed alkali per ½ cup (125 ml) of thick dye paste (see pages 62–63)
¼ teaspoon (1.25 ml) Synthrapol (minimum)
Activated print paste (optional)

*Begin with small pieces of fabric, ¼ yard (23 cm) or smaller. As you become comfortable with monoprinting, increase the size of your pieces.

Procedure

1. Cover your padded table with the canvas drop cloth.
2. Stretch the fabric on top of the canvas covering your work area. Secure with masking tape or T-pins. ①
3. Fill a wide-mouth container half full with warm (comfortable to the touch) water. Use this to rinse your brushes between color changes.
4. Prepare ½ cup (125 ml) of thick dye paste for each color. Pour each color of thick dye paste into a wide-mouth container. The dye paste should be the consistency of honey. For lighter values, dilute the dye paste with activated print paste.

5. Prepare the mixed alkali. Add ½ teaspoon (2 g) of the mixed alkali powder to each ½ cup (125 ml) of thick dye paste. Stir until the powder dissolves. Note the time; discard the dye paste after 4 hours.

6. Using artists' brushes or a wide sponge brush or sponge roller, apply a thin layer of dye paste onto the acrylic square, your printing plate. Saturate the brush or roller evenly, using strokes that cross each other to ensure a uniform surface. If you are too generous with the dye paste, the image will smudge and blur when you transfer the design. Using your fingers and/or other tools, draw on the painted surface. Reverse letters and numbers. **2**

7. Carefully place the printing plate, dye side down, on the fabric. Walk the palms of your hands over the back of the square to transfer the design. **3**

8. Without sliding the printing plate, carefully peel up one edge and lift the plate off the fabric. This is the first layer of your print. **4** **5**

2

3

4

5

Experimenting with Monoprinting

Try one of the following.

- For different textures, apply dye paste with rumpled fabric, a paper towel, a cake-decorating edge tool, a tool for laying tile cement, a plastic comb, a teasing comb, or a sponge. Use your imagination.

- Place the printing plate on the fabric, paint side down, then flip the two over so the fabric is on top. Using a blunt-tipped tool, draw on the fabric. Remember to reverse letters and numbers.

- For a veinlike pattern, paint a thin layer of dye paste onto the printing plate. Lay the fabric on top of the plate, and lightly pat the two. Peel the fabric off the printing plate and set it aside to cure.

- For a feathery pattern, lightly sponge dye paste onto the printing plate.

- For a subtle variation, place leaves or paper shapes onto the painted printing plate before placing it on the fabric, then print. For the second print, brush more dye paste over the leaves or paper.

- Print on dry, damp, or wet fabric.

9. Wipe excess dye paste off the surface of the square. Repeat steps 6–8 with a different color of dye paste. You can print over the first design or on a clean area of the fabric. Do not allow the first print to dry before you print again. The thickener in the dye paste may act as a resist if it dries.

10. Allow the fabric to cure at a temperature **above 70° F (21° C)** for a minimum of 24 hours. See page 62 for ways to maintain the curing temperature.

11. After curing, rinse and wash the fabric by hand or machine. To rinse and wash by hand, fill the plastic bucket half full with 65° to 75° F (18° to 24° C) water. Untape or unpin the fabric and immerse it in the bucket of rinse water. Swish the fabric around the bucket for 1 to 2 minutes. Remove the fabric and change the rinse water. Repeat this rinse 3 to 4 times. You may want to use 2 rinse buckets; the second bucket will be ready and waiting when it is time to change water. When the fabric feels squeaky clean (not soapy), remove it and empty the rinse bucket. (It's okay if you still see color in the rinse water, so long as the fabric feels squeaky clean.) Refill the bucket with 140° F (60° C) water. Add ¼ teaspoon (1.25 ml) of Synthrapol per yard of fabric. Return the fabric to the bucket and swish it around for 5 minutes. Rinse the fabric in warm (comfortable to the touch) water.

    To rinse and wash the fabric by machine, set your washing machine on the small load, warm wash, and warm rinse cycles. After the machine fills and begins to agitate, carefully untape or unpin the fabric and add it to the machine. Close the lid and let the machine continue through the wash, rinse, and spin cycles. After the final spin cycle, reset the machine on the hot wash and warm rinse cycles. After the machine fills with water, add ¼ teaspoon (1.25 ml) of Synthrapol per yard of fabric and let the machine continue through all the cycles. Check the last rinse cycle. If the rinse water is colored, you may need to repeat this step. For dark colors, 2 short wash treatments may work better than 1 long wash.

12. Dry the fabric in a clothes dryer or on a clothesline. Follow the dryer manufacturer's instructions for the appropriate heat setting.

13. Clean up, using the cellulose sponge, rags, or paper towels.

STAMPING

Stamping is an easy introduction to creating a repeat pattern. Stamped patterns can be simple or complex, made with common household items or purchased stamps.

Basically, a stamp is any object that you can paint and apply to fabric. Look around your house—inside and outside—for ideas. You can stamp with or make stamps from corks, empty thread spools, kitchen utensils, string, screw heads, erasers, carved or cut vegetables such as potatoes or green peppers, leaves, cellulose sponges, and bunched-up paper towels. I like to create stamp designs with foam weather stripping and small acrylic squares (see page 118). Be sure to take careful notes so you can re-create or expand on your work later.

Use this recipe to stamp 1 yard (91 cm) of 100% cotton muslin. I recommend adding mixed alkali to the dye paste. Stamping generally creates patterns with a fairly open, light background. The mixed-alkali method leaves less alkali residue than the activator soak, so the dye is easier to rinse out and less likely to stain the light areas.

Read through the directions and assemble all the necessary equipment and supplies before you begin. Wear a dust/mist mask or respirator while working with dye powder and auxiliary products, and remember to wear rubber gloves when you work with the fabric and liquid dye.

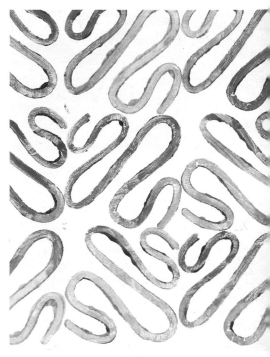

Stamped Fabric

Equipment

2-gallon (8-L) plastic bucket (optional)
Artists' brushes (brights)
Assortment of wide-mouth plastic containers with lids (one for each color you want to use and one for rinsing the brushes)
Canvas drop cloth
Cellulose sponge, rags, or paper towels
Clothesline and clothespins (optional)
Masking tape or T-pins
Measuring cups and spoons or scale
Mixing box (see page 35)
Newspapers
Padded table
Rubber gloves
Soap and old toothbrush for cleaning the stamp(s)
Stamp(s) (see page 118)
Stirring tools
Thermometer
Watch or clock

Helpful Hint

Stamping Variations

Experiment with stamping designs, referring to the examples below and at right. Use different colors and different stamps. Build up layers of color and pattern to create a complex, textured look. Stamp 2 or 3 prints before repainting. The change in value is more interesting than a perfect print.

Supplies

1 yard (91 cm) scoured, 100% cotton muslin (see pages 22–24)*
½ cup (125 ml) each of at least 2 colors of thick dye paste (see pages 58–60)
½ teaspoon (2 g) mixed alkali per ½ cup (125 ml) of thick dye paste (see pages 62–63)
¼ teaspoon (1.25 ml) Synthrapol (minimum)

*Begin with small pieces of fabric, ¼ yard (23 cm) or smaller. As you become comfortable with stamping, increase the size of your pieces.

Procedure

1. Cover your padded table with the canvas drop cloth.
2. Stretch the fabric on top of the canvas covering your work area. Secure with masking tape or T-pins.
3. Fill a wide-mouth container half full with warm (comfortable to the touch) water. Use this to rinse your brush.
4. Prepare ½ cup (125 ml) of thick dye paste for each color you want to use. Pour each color into a wide-mouth container.
5. Prepare the mixed alkali. Add ½ teaspoon (2 g) of the mixed alkali powder to each ½ cup (125 ml) of dye paste. Stir until the powder dissolves. Note the time; discard the dye paste after 4 hours.
6. Using an artists' bright (flat brush), spread a thin layer (1 or 2 colors) of prepared dye paste on the stamp surface. Test the stamp on a piece of paper or scrap of fabric. The amount of dye paste that transfers from the stamp to the fabric depends on how much dye paste is on the stamp and the amount of pressure you use. **1**
7. Stamp your fabric with an all-over, spot, random, or border pattern, as desired. See the illustrations for ideas.

   Allow the fabric to cure at a temperature **above 70° F (21° C)** for a minimum of 24 hours. See page 62 for ways to maintain the proper temperature.

8. Clean all stamps with warm water and soap. Use an old toothbrush to coax dye out of crevices.

9. After curing, rinse and wash the fabric by hand or machine. To rinse and wash by hand, fill the plastic bucket half full with 65° to 75°F (18° to 24°C) water. Untape or unpin the fabric and immerse it in the bucket of rinse water. Swish the fabric around the bucket for 1 to 2 minutes. Remove the fabric and change the rinse water. Repeat this rinse 3 to 4 times. You may want to use 2 rinse buckets; the second bucket will be ready and waiting when it is time to change water. When the fabric feels squeaky clean (not soapy), remove it and empty the rinse bucket. (It's okay if you still see color in the rinse water, so long as the fabric feels squeaky clean.) Refill the bucket with 140°F (60°C) water. Add ¼ teaspoon (1.25 ml) of Synthrapol per yard of fabric. Return the fabric to the bucket and swish it around for 5 minutes. Rinse the fabric in warm (comfortable to the touch) water.

   To rinse and wash the fabric by machine, set your washing machine on the small load, warm wash, and warm rinse cycles. After the machine fills and begins to agitate, carefully untape the fabric and add it to the machine. Close the lid and let the machine continue through the wash, rinse, and spin cycles. After the final spin cycle, reset the machine on the hot wash and warm rinse cycles. After the machine fills with water, add ¼ teaspoon (1.25 ml) of Synthrapol per yard of fabric and let the machine continue through all the cycles. Check the last rinse cycle. If the rinse water is colored, you may need to repeat this step. For dark colors, 2 short wash treatments may work better than 1 long wash.

10. Dry the fabric in a clothes dryer or on a clothesline. Follow the dryer manufacturer's instructions for the appropriate heat setting.

11. Clean up, using the cellulose sponge, rags, or paper towels.

Experimenting with Stamping

The following methods for loading stamps with dye paste are good for stamps with large, bold surfaces. (Detailed surfaces easily fill with paste, and you lose the design.)

- With an acrylic or sponge brush, spread a thin layer of prepared dye paste on a plastic or Styrofoam plate. Dip the stamp in the paste, then stamp the fabric.

- On a plastic or Styrofoam plate, saturate a piece of thin (¼" thick) foam, sponge, or felt with dye paste. Stamp on the saturated material, then stamp the fabric.

- With a foam brush, paint a thin layer of dye paste directly on the stamp surface. Stamp the fabric.

- Try Karen Perrine's method: use a small foam roller to paint stamps with a large surface area. Be careful not to load the roller too full.

MAKING STAMPS

I like to make stamps by attaching pieces of foam weather stripping to a piece of clear acrylic. These stamps take the guesswork out of patterning fabric because you can see the design as you work.

Equipment and Supplies

Several 2" x 2" (5 cm x 5 cm) or slightly larger squares of clear acrylic or Plexiglas

Scissors

Foam weather stripping with adhesive back (You can also use camper mounting tape, Super Glue, foot and shoe padding, or a hot glue gun and an absorbent material, such as ⅛"-thick (3 mm) foam pad or shoe padding.)

Procedure

1. Cut out pieces of foam weather stripping with scissors. **1**
2. Create stamp designs by peeling the adhesive backing off the pieces of foam and attaching them to the acrylic squares. **2**
3. To make a handle, cut a 3" (7.6 cm) -long piece of masking tape and fold it in half; then attach it to the back side of the acrylic square with 2 smaller pieces of masking tape.

1

2

Using Liquid Resists

In addition to the folding and binding techniques on pages 85–88 and 102–5, you can use *liquid* resists to prevent dye from penetrating and coloring fabric. Liquid resists are based on water, solvent, or wax. This book focuses on water-based resists, which are the safest and most convenient for the home dyer. Solvent- and wax-based resists are associated with potential health concerns, and are not addressed in this book.

Water-based resists work best with direct-application techniques that use dye-stock solution and mixed-alkali fixative. You apply the resist to fabric, allow it to dry, paint or stamp dye up to the resist, allow the dye to cure, then rinse the fabric. The area protected by the resist remains the undyed color.

Water-based resists include Sabra Silk, Presist, Silkpaint Brand Water-Soluble Resist, and gutta. (See "Resources" on page 158.) Many water-based resists are clear, but pigment gutta is available in a range of glossy and pearlescent colors that are easy to see. (*Note*: Pigment gutta will change the hand of the fabric.)

You cannot use water-based resists in an immersion dye bath; they will dissolve. Also, if you are working in high humidity or in a damp area, the resist may not completely dry. This will diminish its effectiveness.

There are many ways to apply liquid resist, including painting, stamping, and screen printing. Different resists work better with different techniques. The following recipes use two resists—Sabra Silk for traditional silk-painting techniques and Presist for stamping an image.

The best way to apply a liquid resist to fabric is to stretch the fabric taut and elevate it above the table surface. Use an artists' stretcher frame, silk-painting frame, or embroidery hoop to elevate the fabric. Use T-pins to secure lengths of fabric between two sawhorses. When the fabric gets wet and stretches, there will be no need to unpin. Just move the sawhorses to take the sag out of the fabric.

Fabric Hand Painted with a Resist
and Dye-Stock Solution

HAND PAINTING WITH A RESIST

This recipe applies traditional silk-painting techniques to cotton. Before you begin, plan your design. Then, use the resist to trace or draw your design on fabric. The resist line does not have to be thick, but it must penetrate the fabric to prevent dye from flowing into other areas. Be sure to check the back of the fabric as described below. For more information on silk painting, refer to "Further Reading" on pages 159–60. If you don't want to create an original design, Dover publishes great books of copyright-free images.

You can use any fabric with this recipe, but lightweight fabrics, such as silk and light cotton, tend to be most successful. You may want to experiment on fabric scraps.

Use this recipe to hand paint 1 yard (91 cm) of 100% cotton muslin. I recommend adding mixed alkali to the dye-stock solution.

Read through the directions and assemble all the necessary equipment and supplies before you begin. Wear a dust/mist mask or respirator while working with dye powder and auxiliary products, and remember to wear rubber gloves when you work with the fabric and liquid dye.

Equipment

2-gallon (8-L) plastic bucket (optional)

Artists' brushes: Rounds (#0, #2, #6, and #8) for small areas;
Brights (#6 and #8) for large areas

Artists' stretcher frame, embroidery hoop, or silk-painting frame

Assortment of wide-mouth plastic containers with lids
(one for each color you want to use and one for rinsing the brushes)

Cellulose sponge, rags, or paper towels

Clothesline and clothespins (optional)

Cotton swabs

Fine-line applicator bottles or squeeze bottles
(optional: most water-based resists are sold in these types of bottles)

Masking tape or T-pins

Measuring cups and spoons or scale

Mixing box (see page 35)

Newspapers

Original designs and/or copyright-free images

Plastic drop cloth

Rubber gloves

Soft drawing pencil

Stirring tools

Thermometer

Watch or clock

Supplies

1 yard (91 cm) scoured, 100% cotton muslin (see pages 22–24)*
1/2 cup (125 ml) each of at least 3 colors of dye-stock solution (see pages 50–52)
½ teaspoon (2 g) mixed alkali per ½ cup (125 ml) of dye-stock solution (see pages 62–63)
¼ teaspoon (1.25 ml) Synthrapol (minimum)
Sabra Silk resist

*Begin with small pieces of fabric, ¼ yard (23 cm) or smaller. As you become comfortable with hand painting, increase the size of your pieces.

Procedure

1. Cover your work table with the plastic drop cloth.
2. Using the soft pencil, draw or transfer a design to your fabric. You may want to make a light table to help you transfer the design. Lay a piece of glass or translucent plastic between 2 tables (or on a table with the leaf removed) and place a lamp underneath.

   You can also use a window or a sliding glass door. Tape the pattern to the glass surface; then center the fabric over the pattern. Pull the fabric taut (but not taut enough to stretch the fabric) and tape it to the glass.
3. Stretch the fabric on an artists' stretcher frame, embroidery hoop, or silk-painting frame and secure it with masking tape or T-pins.
4. Place the tip or nozzle of the applicator bottle on one of your pencil lines, pressing the tip firmly against the fabric. Squeeze the bottle gently to force the resist along the line. It is important to maintain an even flow and a continuous line as you trace the design. The dye-stock solution will flow through gaps in the line. **1**

   Check the back of the fabric to make sure the resist penetrated the fabric. The resist should be visible from the back. If you see any gaps in the design, fill them in from the front. You may need to apply the resist to both the front and back of heavy fabric.

   Allow the resist to dry. Hold the fabric up to the light and check again to make sure there are no gaps in the resist before you begin painting. **2**

Helpful Hint

Working with Resists and Dye-Stock Solution

If the dye-stock solution does not flow to the resist line, add a drop of Synthrapol. The Synthrapol helps the solution flow and prevents halos from forming at the edge of the resist line. You can also dampen the fabric slightly, using a sponge dipped in water, but this will dilute the dye color. For lighter values, dilute the dye-stock solution with activated urea water.

Experimenting with an Applied Resist

Try one of the following.

- Blend the colors while the dye-stock solutions are wet.
- Make a colored resist line by adding about ⅜ teaspoon (1g) of dye powder per ½ cup (125 ml) of liquid resist. Color the resist at least one day before using to make sure the dye powder dissolves.
- Sprinkle salt crystals on the design while the dye-stock solution is wet. The salt crystal absorbs the dye, creating darker spots with light-colored halos. Different kinds of salt and different sizes of salt crystal produce different effects. In general, the larger the crystal, the more dramatic the effect.
- Use T-pins to secure lengths of fabric between two sawhorses. When the fabric gets wet and stretches there will be no need to unpin. Just move the sawhorses to take the sag out of the fabric.

5. Prepare ½ cup (125 ml) of dye-stock solution for each color you want to use. When the dye is completely dissolved, pour each solution into a wide-mouth container.

6. Prepare the mixed alkali. Add ½ teaspoon (2 g) of the mixed alkali powder to each ½ cup (125 ml) of dye-stock solution. Stir until the powder dissolves. Note the time; discard the dye-stock solution after 4 hours.

7. Fill a wide-mouth container half full with warm (comfortable to the touch) water. Use this to rinse your brushes.

8. To paint the design, fill an artists' brush with one of the dye-stock solutions prepared in steps 5–6. Touch the brush to the center of an enclosed area. Allow the dye-stock solution to flow to the resist line. Add dye-stock solution as needed to fill the enclosed area. Repeat this process to complete the design. **3**

Work quickly to prevent the dye from drying before you have all your color applied to an area. Do not paint up to the edges or paint on top of the resist line. If you apply too much dye-stock solution, it will pool and may flow into other areas or soak through the resist line. Use a dry brush or cotton swab to mop up dye pools. Remember to rinse your brushes before you use a new color.

9. Allow the fabric to cure at a temperature **above 70° F (21° C)** for a minimum of 24 hours. See page 62 for ways to maintain the curing temperature.

10. After curing, rinse and wash the fabric by hand or machine. To rinse and wash by hand, fill the plastic bucket half full with 65° to 75° F (18° to 24° C) water. Remove the fabric from the artists' stretcher frame and immerse it in the bucket of rinse water. Swish the fabric around the bucket for 1 to 2 minutes. Remove the fabric and change the rinse water. Repeat this rinse 3 to 4 times. You may want to use 2 rinse buckets; the second bucket will be ready and waiting when it is time to change water. When the fabric feels squeaky clean (not soapy), remove it and empty the rinse bucket. (It's okay if you still see color in the rinse water, so long as the fabric feels squeaky clean.) Refill the bucket with 140° F (60° C) water. Add ¼ teaspoon (1.25 ml) of Synthrapol per yard of fabric. Return the fabric to the bucket and swish it around for 5 minutes. Rinse the fabric in warm (comfortable to the touch) water.

To rinse and wash the fabric by machine, set your washing machine on the small load, warm wash, and warm rinse cycles. After the machine fills and begins to agitate, remove the fabric from the artists' stretcher frame and add it to the machine. Close the lid and let the machine continue through the wash, rinse, and spin cycles. After the final spin cycle, reset the machine on the hot wash and warm rinse cycles. After the machine fills with water, add ¼ teaspoon (1.25 ml) of Synthrapol per yard of fabric and let the machine continue through all the cycles. Check the last rinse cycle. If the rinse water is colored, you may need to repeat this step. For dark colors, 2 short wash treatments may work better than 1 long wash.

11. Dry the fabric in a clothes dryer or on a clothesline. Follow the dryer manufacturer's instructions for the appropriate heat setting.

12. Clean up, using the cellulose sponge, rags, or paper towels.

STAMPING WITH PRESIST

Use this technique to explore the principles of positive/negative space on 1 yard (91 cm) of 100% cotton muslin. Use Presist to pattern your fabric, then paint the fabric with thick dye paste. I recommend adding mixed alkali to the thickened dye paste.

Read through the directions and assemble all the necessary equipment and supplies before you begin. Wear a dust/mist mask or respirator while working with dye powder and auxiliary products, and remember to wear rubber gloves when you work with the fabric and liquid dye.

Equipment

2-gallon (8-L) plastic bucket (optional)
Artists' (#12) or sponge brush
Artists' stretcher frame or embroidery hoop
Assortment of wide-mouth plastic containers with lids (one for each color you want to use and one for rinsing the brushes)
Cellulose sponge, rags, or paper towels
Clothesline and clothespins (optional)
Masking tape or T-pins
Measuring cups and spoons or scale
Mixing box (see page 35)
Newspapers
Plastic drop cloth
Plastic or Styrofoam plates
Rubber gloves
Scissors
Spatula
Stamp(s)
Stirring tools
Thermometer
Watch or clock

Fabric Stamped with Presist and Painted with Dye Paste

Making Sponge Stamps

Use a sponge stamp for large images. With a felt-tip marker, draw a design on a dry sponge. Cut out the design with an X-Acto knife or scissors. Attach the cut-out to clear acrylic with a hot glue gun. Look for sponges with different textures for added visual interest.

Experimenting with Presist

Try one of the following.

- Substitute thinned textile paints for dye. Heat set, using a pressing cloth, before rinsing out the Presist.

- Hand paint designs with Presist, then apply dye or textile paints.

Supplies

1 yard (91 cm) scoured, 100% cotton muslin (see pages 22–24)*
Presist
½ cup (125 ml) each of at least 2 colors of thick dye paste (see pages 58–60)
½ teaspoon (2 g) mixed alkali per ½ cup (125 ml) of dye-stock solution (see pages 62–63)
¼ teaspoon (1.25 ml) Synthrapol (minimum)

*Begin with small pieces of fabric, ¼ yard (23 cm) or smaller. As you become comfortable with stamping, increase the size of your pieces.

Procedure

1. Cover your work table with the plastic drop cloth.
2. Stretch the fabric on the artists' stretcher frame or embroidery hoop and secure.
3. Using the spatula, spread a thin layer of Presist on a plastic or Styrofoam plate and dip your stamp in it, or use a sponge brush to apply a layer of Presist to the stamp. (If you are using a sponge stamp, dampen the stamp and wring out excess water before using.) Reload the stamp after each print as you pattern the fabric. When you have completed your design, allow the Presist to air dry. **1**
4. Prepare ½ cup (125 ml) of thick dye paste for each color you want to use. Pour each color of paste into a wide-mouth container.
5. Prepare the mixed alkali. Add ½ teaspoon (2 g) of the mixed alkali powder to each ½ cup (125 ml) of dye paste. Stir until the powder dissolves. Note the time; discard the prepared paste after 4 hours.
6. Fill a wide-mouth container half full with warm (comfortable to the touch) water. Use this to rinse your brushes.
7. Using an artists' or sponge brush and long strokes, apply 1 color to the stretched fabric. Apply additional colors, blending as

1

desired. Wipe excess dye paste off patterned Presist areas. If you don't wipe off the dye paste, the Presist will dissolve and the dye will penetrate to the fabric. **2**

8. Allow the fabric to cure at a temperature **above 70° F (21° C)** for a minimum of 24 hours. See page 62 for ways to maintain the curing temperature.

9. After curing, rinse and wash the fabric by hand or machine. To rinse and wash by hand, fill the plastic bucket half full with 65° to 75° F (18° to 24° C) water. Remove the fabric from the artists' stretcher frame and immerse it in the bucket of rinse water. Swish the fabric around the bucket for 1 to 2 minutes. Remove the fabric and change the rinse water. Repeat this rinse 3 to 4 times. You may want to use 2 rinse buckets; the second bucket will be ready and waiting when it is time to change water. When the fabric feels squeaky clean (not soapy), remove it and empty the rinse bucket. (It's okay if you still see color in the rinse water, so long as the fabric feels squeaky clean.) Refill the bucket with 140° F (60° C) water. Add ¼ teaspoon (1.25 ml) of Synthrapol per yard of fabric. Return the fabric to the bucket and swish it around for 5 minutes. Rinse the fabric in warm (comfortable to the touch) water.

To rinse and wash the fabric by machine, set your washing machine on the small load, warm wash, and warm rinse cycles. After the machine fills and begins to agitate, remove the fabric from the artists' stretcher frame and add it to the machine. Close the lid and let the machine continue through the wash, rinse, and spin cycles. After the final spin cycle, reset the machine on the hot wash and warm rinse cycles. After the machine fills with water, add ¼ teaspoon (1.25 ml) of Synthrapol per yard of fabric and let the machine continue through all the cycles. Check the last rinse cycle. If there is still Presist on the fabric or if the rinse water is colored, you may need to repeat this step. For dark colors, 2 short wash treatments may work better than 1 long wash.

Alternative Curing Methods for Dyes

The direct-application dyeing recipes include fixing-agent and curing instructions, but you may want to try one of the following alternatives as you become more experienced.

Baking Soda Fixative: I do not recommend this method for silk. Add 1 teaspoon (4 g) baking soda per cup (250 ml) of dye-stock solution or dye paste. To cure, choose one of the following: air dry fabric then steam set for 15 minutes, dry fabric in a clothes dryer for 45 minutes on the hottest setting, or preheat your oven to 275° F (135° C), then bake fabric for 2 to 5 minutes. Rinse and wash as directed in the direct-application dyeing recipes.

Citric Acid Crystals: This method is for curing silk only. Add 1 teaspoon (5.8 g) citric acid crystals per cup (250 ml) of dye-stock solution or dye paste. To cure, cover fabric with plastic for 24 hours in a 70°F (21°C) room (minimum temperature), or steam set fabric for 15 minutes. Rinse and wash as instructed in the direct-application dyeing recipes.

2

1

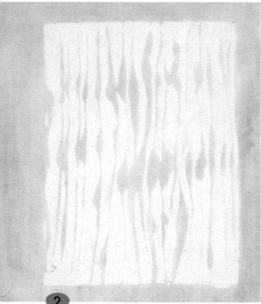

2

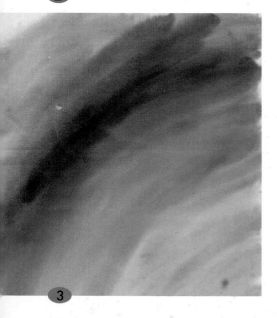

3

10. Dry the fabric in a clothes dryer or on a clothesline. Follow the dryer manufacturer's instructions for the appropriate heat setting.
11. Clean up, using the cellulose sponge, rags, or paper towels.

TROUBLESHOOTING

Light or white areas in the pattern are stained. 1

The fabric was not properly rinsed. Use 65° to 75°F (18° to 24°C) rinse water only and agitate continuously for the first two rinses. You may be able to remove stains by washing the fabric again in 140° to 160°F (60° to 71°C) water with ¼ teaspoon (1.25 ml) of Synthrapol per yard of fabric.

The color is not as bright as it should be and the dye washes off in the rinse water. 2

There are six possible causes: there may not have been enough dye, the water used to dissolve the dye may have been too hot, there may be a finish on the fabric, the curing temperature may have been too low, the dye-stock solution was too old, and/or you forgot to add fixative.

You may have to work through a process of elimination: use more dye; check the temperature of the water used to dissolve the dye powder; check the curing temperature; or do the water-drop test (see page 24), scour the fabric again, use different fabric, or mix fresh dye-stock solution.

The fabric did not dye evenly. 3

The fabric was not correctly scoured or the activator soak was not evenly applied. Scour the fabric again or use another fabric that has been scoured. When you place the fabric in the activator soak, it should be completely submerged and able to move freely.

▲ *Remember the Chalice*
by Natasha Kempers-Cullen, 1993,
Topsham, Maine, 81" x 102". **Method**:
Fiber-reactive dye and textile paint on cotton.
Hand painted and stamped. Machine
pieced and hand quilted. Hand embroidered
and embellished with beads, semiprecious
stones, and fetishes. Photo by Dennis Griggs.

❯ *Saints and Sinners: Revelations*
by Natasha Kempers-Cullen, 1996,
Topsham, Maine, 48" x 48". **Method**:
Fiber-reactive dye and textile paint on cotton.
Hand painted and printed. Machine pieced
and hand quilted and beaded. Photo by
Dennis Griggs.

∧ *Caterpillar Hill*
by Elizabeth A. Busch, 1991,
Glenburn, Maine, 32" x 33".
Method: Fiber-reactive dye and textile
paint on cotton. Hand painted and
monoprinted. Machine pieced and
quilted. Photo by Dennis Griggs.

❯ *Coping IV*
by Erika Carter, 1997, Bellevue,
Washington, 23½" x 23½".
Method: Textile paint on cotton.
Hand painted. Machine pieced,
appliquéd, and quilted. Photo by
Howard Carter.

< *Parameters: Window*
by Erika Carter, 1994, Bellevue,
Washington, 58" x 58". **Method**:
Textile paint on cotton. Hand painted.
Machine pieced and quilted. Photo
by Howard Carter.

∨ *Persephone's Dream*
by Elizabeth A. Busch, 1993,
Glenburn, Maine, 34" x 27½".
Method: Fiber-reactive dye and
textile paint on cotton. Hand painted.
Machine pieced and hand quilted
and embroidered. Photo by Dennis
Griggs.

▲ *Medicine Lodge*
by Gayle Fraas and Duncan Slade,
1994, Edgecomb, Maine,
60" x 60". **Method**: Whole-cloth
quilt. Fiber-reactive dye on cotton.
Hand painted and printed. Machine
and hand quilted by the artists.
Embellished with foil. Photo by
Dennis Griggs.

▶ *Leaves 2*
by Ann Johnston, 1995, Lake
Oswego, Oregon, 48" x 48".
Method: Fiber-reactive dye on
cotton. Patterned with resist.
Machine pieced and quilted.
Photo by Bill Bachhuber.

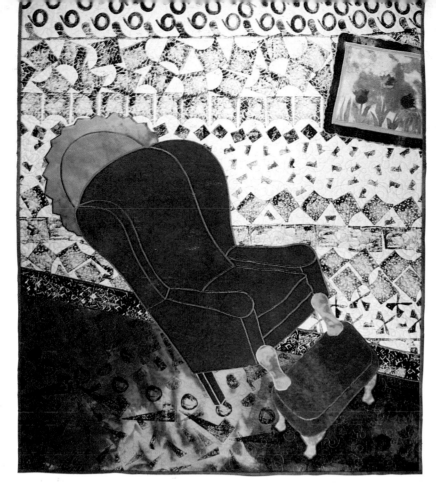

◀ *Nude Blue Chair Reclining*
by Laura Wasilowski, 1996, Elgin, Illinois,
42" x 50". **Method**: Fiber-reactive dye on cotton.
Hand dyed and stamped. Machine pieced,
appliquéd, and quilted. Photo by Melody
Johnson.

▽ *Gives Me the Hee Bee Gee Bees*
by Laura Wasilowski, 1994, Elgin, Illinois,
50½" x 49". **Method**: Fiber-reactive dye on
cotton. Hand dyed, stamped, screen printed, and
painted. Machine pieced and quilted. Photo by
Melody Johnson.

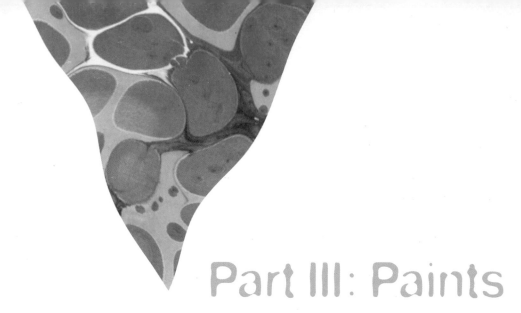

Part III: Paints

Textile paints are fun to use because they are easy to apply and they produce immediate results. Like fiber-reactive dyes, paints can be thick (like jelly), thin (like water), or any consistency in between. You can thin textile paints to paint washes of color and to produce elaborate marbled patterns.

The different types of textile paints include transparent, opaque, and pearlescent. Some transparent paints behave like dyes; you can blend colors, and the value becomes darker as you apply more layers. Opaque paints, in most cases, do not change in value as you apply layers. You can use opaque paints to obscure the color or pattern already on the fabric and to apply color or pattern to dark fabric. Pearlescent paints add both color and sparkle. For a hint of shimmer, mix a small amount of pearlescent paint with another color. You can also dilute pearlescent paint to paint a color wash (see pages 106–8).

All textile paints contain finely ground particles of color that are not soluble in water. They are, in essence, glued to fabric with binders or adhesives. The binders adhere to almost any kind of fabric, including synthetic blends.

Common brands of textile paint include Setacolor, PROfab Textile Ink, Versatex, Lumiere, Neopaque, and Deka. (See "Resources" on page 158.) You can mix the colors and types of paint within each brand. Different manufacturers use different binders or adhesives. These adhesives can alter the hand and drape of fabric. Test several brands before investing in large quantities of any one. (I like using Setacolor transparent textile paints for white or light-colored fabric and Setacolor opaque textile paints for dark fabric. This brand offers a wide range of colors and does not leave a heavy residue on the fabric.)

Fabric colored with textile paints is resistant to fading from exposure to light and dry cleaning. However, these paints are known for their tendency to crock (rub off) with repeated or harsh wash and wear. To extend the life of an image on a garment, turn the garment inside out when laundering.

Textile paints are nontoxic, but they do have an odor that some people find objectionable. Always work in a well-ventilated area.

We must always remember that a *method* is neither creative nor uncreative: it is the artist's *mind* that creates.

Susan Bosence

Equipment

The following is a general overview of the equipment needed for working with textile-paint techniques. Some of this equipment is the same as that needed for working with fiber-reactive dyes. Browse yard sales, hardware stores, dye suppliers, art suppliers, and craft stores for equipment you do not have at home. A list of what is absolutely necessary is included at the beginning of each recipe.

Containers: Use assorted sizes of wide-mouth plastic or glass containers with tightly fitting lids for mixing, rinsing brushes, and storing textile paints. You will also need one-quart (1-L), two-gallon (8-L), and five-gallon (20-L) containers or buckets. Refer to the recipes for specific requirements.

Measuring cup: Both plastic cups and Pyrex glassware are suitable. Some suppliers offer plastic safety beakers with markings. You need a one-cup (250 ml) measure.

Measuring spoons: You need a set of plastic or stainless steel measuring spoons.

Mixing box: See the directions for making a mixing box on page 35. Use a mixing box when measuring the activator for scouring.

Newspaper and/or plastic drop cloth: You'll want to cover your workspace with something to protect it from stains.

See the directions for making a mixing box on page 35.

Helpful Hint

Using Fiber-Reactive Dyes in the Textile-Paint Recipes

With the exceptions of sun printing and marbling, you can use fiber-reactive dyes instead of textile paints with any of the techniques in this section. Prepare scoured, 100% cotton muslin in activator soak or add mixed alkali to the dye-stock solution or paste. Mix dye-stock solution, adding print paste if you want to thicken the consistency. Pattern the fabric as described in the textile-paint recipe; then cure and wash as described in the direct-application recipes.

Textile Painting Equipment

Rubber gloves: You can use disposable latex or reusable rubber gloves. Make sure they fit well so you will be comfortable.

Scale: There are many different types of scales available (for example, kitchen, digital, counterbalance, and triple-beam). Choose a scale that you find easy to use. Make sure that it is accurate. A scale that measures from 1 gram to 2 pounds is handy. Use a bathroom scale to weigh large amounts of fabric. (Weigh yourself while holding the dry fabric; then weigh yourself without the fabric. The difference is the weight of the fabric.)

Shallow tray: For marbling, I recommend a white, 2" to 3" (5 to 7.6 cm) deep tray that is slightly longer and wider than the fabric you plan to marble. A good size to begin with is 10" x 10" (25 cm x 25 cm). It's important that the tray be white or another light color so you can clearly see the marbling colors on the surface of the prepared size.

You can make a simple tray by cutting down a cardboard box and covering it with a white plastic garbage bag.

Stirring tools: You need several small spoons, swizzle sticks, or wooden tongue depressors. You may find a wire whisk and rubber scraper or spatula helpful.

Thermometer: You can use any kind of thermometer, as long as it measures to 140° F (60° C).

Timer: You need a kitchen timer, watch, or clock.

Tools that are useful for specific techniques include: pushpins and/or masking tape; Styrofoam plates or plastic trays; foam pad; artists' stretcher frame or embroidery hoop; assorted artists', sponge, and stencil brushes; assorted sizes of squeeze bottles and/or syringes; rubber or acrylic stamps; cellulose sponges; index cards or precut stencils; an X-Acto or other sharp knife; a marbling rake, hair stylus, teasing comb, or cardboard and toothpicks; a clothesline and plastic clothespins; and rags, old towels, or paper towels.

Supplies

Alum (potassium aluminum sulfate): This chemical acts like a magnet, picking up the marbling colors that float on the size. If fabric is not prepared with alum, the colors will not adhere to the fabric. You can purchase alum that is appropriate for marbling through mail-order companies that specialize in dye supplies (see page 158). Follow the mixing instructions provided by the manufacturer.

Store alum in a cool, dry place. Keep it in a container with a tightly fitting lid. You can continue using the alum as long as you are able to dissolve it.

Clear household ammonia: Thicken methyl cellulose size with clear household ammonia that contains clear ammonia or ammonium hydroxide solution. Avoid products that contain alcohol, nonionic surfactant, perfume, detergent, or color. These will disrupt the surface tension of the size, and the marbling colors will not float. If the ammonia is old, the size will not thicken.

Distilled water: If you have hard water, use only distilled water to mix your size.

Methyl cellulose: There are many different thickeners used for size: methyl cellulose, carrageenan or Irish moss tea (seaweed), wallpaper paste, liquid starch, gelatin, and marbling medium. I recommend methyl cellulose because it produces a very smooth surface, is easy to prepare, has a long shelf life (once prepared), and is less expensive than other types of size. Also, methyl cellulose is biodegradable and can be poured down the drain into any septic or city disposal system.

Prepared methyl cellulose lasts longer if made with distilled water. I have stored it in a plastic bucket with a tightly fitting lid for more than six months. As methyl cellulose degrades, the consistency becomes thinner.

Marbling colors: Although you can thin many water-based textile paints for marbling, I recommend purchasing paints that have been prepared for marbling. Preparing marbling colors from textile paints can be a time-consuming process. Fabric marbling kits are available from art and craft stores and mail-order suppliers.

Store marbling colors in a cool, dry place. Secure lids tightly. You can use marbling colors as long as they have not dried out or been frozen.

Marbling surfactant: This is the surface active agent responsible for changing the surface tension of marbling colors. Marbling surfactant is added to the marbling colors to facilitate spreading or floating of the colors. Surfactants include Synthrapol, dish washing liquid, rubbing alcohol, and products made specifically for marbling. For best results, I recommend marbling surfactants that are designed for marbling.

Store marbling surfactant with your marbling colors in a cool, dry place. You can use marbling surfactant as long as it has not dried out or been frozen.

Textile paints: There are transparent, opaque, and pearlescent paints. Common brands include Setacolor, PROfab Textile Ink, Versatex, Lumiere, Neopaque, and Deka.

Textile Paints

I like using Setacolor transparent paints for white and light-colored fabric and Setacolor opaque paints for dark fabric. For more information, refer to "Assembling a Palette" on page 136.

Consult the manufacturer for shelf life information. In general, you can use paints as long as they have not dried out or been frozen. If the paint and base separate, stir thoroughly before using (so it is lump-free).

PRO Chem Colorless Extender: This is a marbling color without the color. If you want the fabric color to be part of the design, use colorless extender to create the design.

Heat Setting Textile Paints

Although some textile paints will cure over time, heat setting ensures the colors are permanent. It is important to follow the manufacturer's instructions. Most paints will cure with one of the following methods. Always air dry before heat setting, preferably for twenty-four hours.

- If you are using a cellulose fabric (cotton, linen, viscose rayon, jute, ramie, or any combination of these fibers), you can heat-set the textile paints with an iron. Iron the fabric on a hot setting (cotton/linen) from the back side for five minutes. You can also place a clean, dry cloth—a "pressing cloth"—over the front of the fabric and iron it for five minutes. Do not use steam. Keep the iron moving to prevent scorching. *Silk is easily scorched, so be sure to use a pressing cloth.*

- Put the painted, air-dried fabric in a commercial clothes dryer for thirty to sixty minutes or in a home clothes dryer for sixty to ninety minutes. Use the hottest setting on the dryer.

- Coil the fabric in a loose roll and place it in an oven for 2 to 3 minutes at 300°F (148°C). Be careful not to scorch the fabric. Remove the fabric from the oven, turn it inside out, and roll it in the opposite direction. Place the fabric in the oven for another 2 to 3 minutes. This method is not recommended for silk, rayon, or other delicate fabrics.

- An old-fashioned mangle—a large press that uses dry heat and pressure—works well. Make sure there is a protective cloth between the hot rollers and the painted fabric.

Store colorless extender in a cool, dry place. You can use colorless extender as long as it has not dried out or been frozen.

Vinegar: Distilled white vinegar is an optional marbling supply. It is necessary only if your water source is very alkaline.

Assembling a Palette

Color mixing with textile paints is much simpler than color mixing with dyes; what you see is what you get. Try mixing small amounts of different-color paints to gain experience. For light colors and values, add a very small amount of the darker color then mix well before adding more. It takes very little paint to darken a light color, but a lot of paint to lighten a dark color.

The textile paint user's palette includes Setacolor Lemon Yellow 17, Setacolor Buttercup 13, Setacolor Vermilion 26, Setacolor Fuchsia 49, Setacolor Ultramarine Blue 12, Setacolor Cobalt Blue 11, Setacolor Black Lake 19, and Setacolor Titanium White 10. If you like adding sparkle to your fabrics, you also need Setacolor Pearl 44. The following colors are referred to by the manufacturer's name and number. The colors shown below are approximate; the actual color may vary slightly.

Textile Paint Palette

Textile Paint Techniques

As you can imagine, there are a multitude of ways to apply textile paints to fabric. This book covers just a few: printing with found objects, stenciling, sun printing, and marbling. For more information, see "Further Reading" on pages 159–60.

STAMPING WITH FOUND OBJECTS

You can use many things to stamp textile paint on fabric: common household items, shaped sponges, purchased stamps, and so on. This easy recipe produces sumptuous natural patterns using the backs of shells and the undersides of leaves.

If you can go to the beach (or have a friend go), pick up shells and pieces of shells. Look for leaves with intriguing shapes and textures. Try to select leaves that are supple, fuzzy, or thick. Avoid young or tender leaves; new growth becomes limp and tears easily, which makes stamping frustrating and messy.

Use this recipe to pattern ½ yard (46 cm) of 100% cotton muslin. Read through the directions and assemble all the necessary equipment and supplies before you begin.

Fabrics Stamped with Found Objects

Equipment

Artists' brushes: Brights (#6 and #12) for large areas

Assortment of shells and/or fresh leaves

Canvas drop cloth (optional)

Cellulose sponge, rags, or paper towels

Foam pad, 1" (2.5 cm) thick for shell printing
(It's easiest when the pad is the same width and length as your fabric.)

Glass cleaner and/or liquid dish soap (optional)

Masking tape

Plastic drop cloth

Rubber gloves (optional)

Wide-mouth plastic container

Resealable plastic sandwich bags (optional)

Supplies

½ yard (46 cm) scoured, 100% cotton muslin (see pages 22–24)

Setacolor transparent or textile paints, at least 4 colors*

*Use opaque textile paints for dark fabrics.

Helpful Hint

Layering Textile Paint

To mix and layer textile paints on fabric, you must work while the paints are wet. New layers will not adhere to dry paint.

Procedure

1. Cover your work table with the plastic drop cloth. If working with shells, lay a piece of foam pad on the drop cloth, then lay your fabric on the pad. If working with leaves, cover your work table with a plastic or canvas drop cloth, then lay your fabric on top. Secure the fabric with masking tape.

2. The shells and leaves must be clean—test by painting them with water. If the water beads up, dry the shell or leaf and spray it with glass cleaner. Pat it dry and test again. You may need to wash slick leaves. Use a drop of liquid dish detergent, then rinse and pat dry.

3. Fill the wide-mouth container half full with warm (comfortable to the touch) water. Use this to rinse your brushes.

4. Using a brush, apply a thin layer of 1 color of textile paint to the round side of a shell or the underside of a leaf. When painting a leaf, start at the center of the leaf and work out to the edges. Make sure the shell or leaf is completely covered with paint. Be careful not to apply too thick a layer of paint; if you use too much, the image will smudge when you press the shell or leaf on the fabric. **1**

5. If you are working with a shell, carefully roll the painted side on the fabric to transfer the image. **2**

   If you are working with a leaf, carefully place the painted side on the fabric. Holding the leaf in place with a finger, cover it with a paper towel. (Don't forget to remove your finger.) Gently walk your fingers over the paper towel to transfer the image. Carefully peel back the paper towel and remove the leaf. **3**

6. Wipe or pat the excess paint off the shell, leaf, or plastic drop cloth. Repeat steps 4 and 5 until the fabric is completely patterned.

   If you change colors, wipe or pat the excess paint off the shell or leaf, then apply the new color.

   Store firm leaves in a resealable plastic bag in your refrigerator. They will remain usable for several days.

7. Allow the fabric to air dry before heat setting it, preferably for 24 hours.

8. See the manufacturer's directions for heat setting. For more information on heat setting, see "Heat Setting Textile Paints" on page 136.

9. Clean up, using the cellulose sponge, rags, or paper towels.

STENCILING

Used to embellish fabric for hundreds of years, stenciling is an easy, versatile technique that lends itself to large patterns. The imagery can be bold and sharp or soft with painstakingly blended colors. Stenciling is a great technique for patterning the border of a garment or a length of fabric. Try using the same design element but gradually varying the colors for interest.

You can purchase or make stencils (see page 140). I prefer to begin with uncomplicated shapes, neither too small nor tightly curved. For more control over the painted image, apply textile paint with a stencil brush, a round brush with stiff, even bristles. For a mottled effect, apply paint with a sponge or sponge roller (for large areas).

Use this recipe to stencil ½ yard (46 cm) of 100% cotton muslin. Read through the directions and assemble all the necessary equipment and supplies before you begin.

Stenciled Fabric

Equipment

Cellulose sponge or rags
Masking tape
Paper towels
Paper or Styrofoam plates
Plastic drop cloth
Rubber gloves (optional)
Stencil(s)
Stencil brushes, ¼" or ½" (0.5 or 1.25 cm), or small natural sponges
Wide-mouth plastic container

Supplies

½ yard (46 cm) scoured, 100% cotton muslin (see pages 22–24)
Setacolor transparent paints, at least 4 colors*

*Use opaque textile paints for dark fabrics.

Procedure

1. Cover your work table with the plastic drop cloth, then lay your fabric on top. Secure the fabric with masking tape.
2. Place a stencil on the fabric and secure with masking tape.
3. Fill the wide-mouth container half full with warm (comfortable to the touch) water. Use this to rinse your brushes.
4. Dip the tip of a brush in paint. Do not overload your brush! Place a paper towel on a paper or Styrofoam plate. Dab the brush on the towel to remove excess paint. The brush should be nearly dry, but moist enough to produce a light stipple effect when you pull it across a sheet of paper. If you use too much paint, it may creep under the edge of the stencil and blur the design.

Making Stencils

You can purchase ready-made stencils at art- and craft-supply stores, or you can design your own. To make a stencil, draw a design on an index card, file folder, or a piece of heavy-gauge plastic. Translating a design to a stencil can be tricky; enclosed shapes must be connected to other shapes with "bridges." Some images may need to be simplified or stylized. Use an X-Acto or other sharp knife to cut out the design. Be sure to cut on a self-healing cutting mat.

To prevent stencils made from paper from degrading, spray them with clear varnish. For more information on making stencils, refer to "Further Reading" on pages 159–60.

5. Hold the brush so the tip is pointed straight down, rather than at an angle. Use a dabbing (or pouncing) motion to color the open areas of the stencil. Work from the outside edges toward the inside. Gradually build up color(s) by applying several layers of paint and/or by blending colors. Allowing the brush to run out of paint as you work gives the design shading and texture. **1**

6. When you have completely filled in the design, remove the masking tape from the edges of the stencil and carefully peel off the stencil. (Be careful not to smudge the paint.) Check the underside of the stencil for paint; remove any excess with a cellulose sponge, rag, or paper towel.

   If you want to pattern the entire fabric, tape the stencil to another area and repeat steps 4–6. Before you place the stencil on top of a patterned area, make sure the paint is dry.

7. Allow the fabric to air dry before heat setting, preferably for 24 hours.

8. See the manufacturer's directions for heat setting. For more information, see "Heat Setting Textile Paints" on page 136.)

9. Clean up, using the cellulose sponge, rags, or paper towels. Place stencils on a flat surface to clean. Try to avoid catching and tearing the edges.

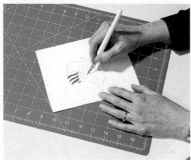

SUN PRINTING

Use stencils, salt, sunshine, and Setacolor transparent textile paints to create luminous colors and patterns on fabric. Setacolor paints are sensitive to sunlight. If the sun isn't cooperative, you can use a halogen lamp, sun lamp with ultraviolet light, or an infrared heat lamp. Sun printing can be tricky in arid regions because the fabric dries too quickly. For best results, work with small pieces of fabric and work as quickly as possible.

Thin Setacolor paints with water so you can apply a color wash, or dip the fabric in a container of diluted paint, then wring the paint out. Lay the fabric in the sun, then cover it with stencils or other objects.

This recipe is for printing ½ yard (46 cm) of 100% cotton muslin. Read through the directions and assemble all the necessary equipment and supplies before you begin.

Sun-Printed Fabric and Baseball Cap

Equipment

Cellulose sponge, rags, or paper towels
Artists' stretcher frame or embroidery hoop
Masking tape or T-pins
Measuring cups and spoons or scale
Plastic drop cloth
Rubber gloves
Stirring tools
Sponge brush, 2" (5 cm) wide
Stencils, leaves, lace, or index-card cutouts (any opaque item)
Wide-mouth containers with lids (one for each color you want to use and one for rinsing the brush)

Supplies

½ yard (46 cm) scoured, 100% cotton muslin (see pages 22–24)
Setacolor transparent or textile paints, at least 2 colors*
Coarse table, kosher, or sea salt

*Begin with small pieces of fabric, 12" x 12" (30 cm x 30 cm), or smaller. As you become comfortable with sun printing, increase the size of your pieces.

Procedure

1. Cover your work table with the plastic drop cloth.
2. Stretch the fabric on an artists' stretcher frame or embroidery hoop and secure it with masking tape or T-pins.
3. Fill a wide-mouth container half full with warm (comfortable to the touch) water. Use this to rinse your brush and moisten your fabric.

4. Dilute the textile paints with water, using the wide-mouth containers for mixing. Begin with 1 part Setacolor paint and 2 parts water. Experiment to determine how much you want to dilute the paint.

5. Paint your fabric, working rapidly. Blend colors as desired.

6. Place the stencils, leaves, lace, or cutouts on the fabric. **1**

7. Sprinkle the fabric with coarse table, kosher, or sea salt. The salt reacts with the paint and sunlight to create halos of color.

8. Place the fabric (still on the artists' stretcher frame or in an embroidery hoop) in sunlight or under a lamp. Leave the fabric in sunlight or under the lamp until it is completely dry; then remove the opaque objects and brush off the salt. **2**

9. See the manufacturer's directions for heat setting. For more information on heat setting, see "Heat Setting Textile Paints" on page 136.)

10. Clean up, using the cellulose sponge, rags, or paper towels.

MARBLING

The graceful lines and intricate patterns of marbling are mesmerizing, and the moment you transfer the pattern is magical. Although the technique requires planning and preparation, the finished result is well worth it. You must prepare the alum soak, fabric, and size (steps 1–6) in advance. Because the fabric must air dry, you may want to split this recipe into 2 days, doing steps 1–6 on the first day, then proceeding through the remaining steps another day.

There are few limits to marbling. Experimenting is essential! You can use white, colored, or patterned fabric for background. In fact, marbling is an excellent way to pattern dyed fabrics that are not up to par. You can even marble a previously marbled image. This is referred to as shadow marbling.

This recipe is based on colors made by PRO Chem specifically for marbling. Although you can thin many water-based textile paints for marbling, I recommend that you purchase colors prepared for marbling. Preparing marbling colors from paints can be a time-consuming process. Fabric-marbling kits are available from art and craft stores and through mail-order suppliers (see page 158).

You can marble any surface that absorbs alum, including fabric, paper, tennis shoes, egg shells, and even wood! For additional information on marbling, refer to "Further Reading" on pages 159–60.

Use this recipe to marble 4 to 5 yards (3.65 to 4.57 m) of 100% cotton fabric. Read through the directions and assemble all the necessary equipment and supplies before you begin. ①

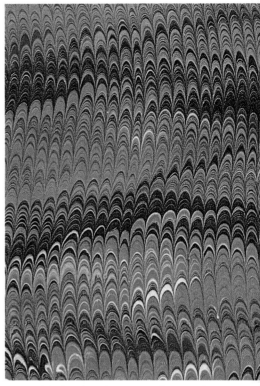

Marbled Fabric (Nonpareil Pattern)

Making a Marbling Rake and Comb

For traditional marbling patterns, you need special rakes and combs that extend the width and length of your marbling tray. To make a marbling rake, cut a piece of cardboard, foam core, or balsa wood 1" (2.5 cm) shorter than the width of your tray. Tape toothpicks or plastic hairpins at 1" (2.5 cm) intervals. To make a marbling comb, cut a piece of cardboard, foam core, or balsa wood 1" (2.5 cm) shorter than the width of your tray. Tape or push long sewing pins through the material at ¼" (6.3 mm) intervals.

Marbled Vest by Judy Simmons, 1997, Marietta, Georgia. Marbled silk lining.

Equipment

1-quart (1-L) plastic measure
5-gallon (20-L) plastic bucket
Two 2-gallon (8-L) plastic buckets with lids
Cellulose sponge, rags, or paper towels
Clothesline and clothespins
Kitchen timer or watch
Measuring cups and spoons or scale
Newspaper (cut to ¼ page)
Plastic drop cloth
Plastic-lined garbage can or plastic trash bag
Rubber gloves (optional)
Scissors
Shallow tray
Stirring tools
Teasing comb, marbling rake, toothpicks, and/or plastic hairpins
Thermometer

Supplies

4 tablespoons (60 g) alum
4 to 5 yards (3.6 to 4.5 m) scoured, 100% cotton muslin (see pages 22–24)
3½ tablespoons (25 g) methyl cellulose M112 powder (for size)
1 teaspoon (5 ml) clear household ammonia
1 gallon (4 L) distilled water, if your water is hard or heavily chlorinated
1 teaspoon (5 ml) distilled white vinegar, if your water is very alkaline
PRO Chem Colorless Extender (optional)
Marbling colors, at least 4
Marbling surfactant

Procedure

Part 1

1. Hang the clothesline and place clothespins nearby. Cover your work area with the plastic drop cloth. Position your shallow tray near the edge of the work table. Place a plastic-lined garbage can or plastic trash bag under the edge of the table to catch drips.

2. To make the alum soak, dissolve 4 tablespoons (60 g) of alum in 1 gallon (4 L) of 120° F (50° C) water. Stir until dissolved.

3. Add scoured fabric (wet or dry) to the alum soak. Soak the fabric for 10 to 15 minutes, stirring intermittently. Make sure the fabric is completely submerged and can move freely in the bucket.

4. Remove the fabric from the bucket. Holding the fabric over the bucket, wring out the excess solution. Do not rinse the fabric!

5. Hang the fabric on a clothesline to dry. Make sure the fabric is not folded or overlapping. Do not use a clothes dryer to dry alum-soaked fabrics; heat tenderizes cotton.

   If necessary, press the line-dried fabric with a cool iron to remove creases. Do not press with a hot iron. When the fabric is dry, cut it to the inside dimensions of your tray.

6. To make the size, measure 1 gallon (4 L) of 75° to 95° F (24° to 35° C) water into the other 2-gallon (8-L) bucket. Add 3½ tablespoons (25 g) of methyl cellulose M112 powder to the bucket. Stir until the methyl cellulose dissolves. While stirring, add 1 teaspoon (5 ml) of clear household ammonia. Continue stirring until the solution begins to look clear (2 to 3 minutes). Stir intermittently for 30 minutes.

   If you have hard or heavily chlorinated water, use distilled water to make the size. The impurities in the water can disrupt the surface tension of the size.

   If you have very alkaline water, add 1 teaspoon (5 ml) of distilled white vinegar to each gallon (4 L) of size.

   The size is ready for marbling. For best results, allow the size to sit for 12 hours or overnight before using. Store the size and marbling colors in the same room at 60° to 80° F (16° to 27° C) before using.

Part 2

1. Fill the 5-gallon (20-L) plastic bucket half full with warm (comfortable to the touch) water.

2. Fill the shallow tray with 1" to 2" (2.5 to 5 cm) of the size.

3. To skim the size, drag a strip of newspaper across the surface of the size, then discard the paper. This evens out the surface tension and clears the bubbles. Do not worry about the bubbles remaining along the edges of the marbling tray. These will not disrupt the pattern. **2**

Helpful Hint

Tips for Using Alum

You can keep the alum soak in a plastic bucket with a tight-fitting lid for 2 to 3 months. Store at room temperature. Alum crystallizes when it is too cold or old. If new alum solution crystallizes, reheat it to dissolve the crystals. Discard old solution. Do not store alum-treated cotton fabric for longer than 2 to 3 weeks before marbling; alum causes cotton fibers to disintegrate.

4. Shake the marbling colors and Colorless Extender (if using) well before each use and periodically during the marbling session. Using a pushpin, make a fine hole in the nozzle of the applicator bottle.

Test each of the marbling colors. Hold the applicator bottle close to the size and squeeze 1 drop of color onto the surface. The marbling color should float and spread out in a circle measuring from ½" to 2" (1.5 to 5 cm) in diameter. If the drop does not spread, add marbling surfactant to the marbling color in the applicator bottle, 2 to 3 drops at a time, and test again. Be careful; you cannot remove the surfactant if you add too much.

Test the colors to make sure they all float together, then skim the surface. **3**

5. To make the marble pattern, carefully squeeze drops of your first color on the size. (Use as many drops as you like.) Using your other marbling colors, repeat this process until you have completely covered the surface. *Note:* The fabric shows through areas not completely covered with marbling color. You can place drops side by side or on top of previous color(s). The more drops, the deeper the color. **4** **5**

3

4

5

6. Using a teasing comb, marbling rake, toothpick, or plastic hairpin, pattern the marbling colors. See the illustrations on page 148 for ideas. **6**

7. Trim all loose threads from the edges of the fabric.

8. Hold 2 opposite corners of the piece of fabric. In one fluid movement, gently lay the middle of the fabric on top of the marbling colors and drop the edges. **7** **8**

9. Remove the fabric from the tray, then immerse it several times in the rinse bucket. Do not rub the fabric. Gently squeeze excess water from the fabric and hang it on the clothesline to dry. **9**

10. Clean up, using the cellulose sponge, rags, or paper towels.

11. Allow the fabric to air dry and cure for 3 days before washing. Some paints need to be heat set. Follow the manufacturer's directions (remember to use a cool iron).

    After the fabric has cured, you can wash it by hand or in a washing machine. Set the machine for the gentlest cycle. Use cool water and mild soap. Rinse the fabric in 75° to 95° F (24° to 35° C) water and hang to dry.

Helpful Hint

Cleaning Equipment

Do not clean your equipment with soap; use water and a stiff brush. Soap residue interferes with surface tension and can cause some of the problems listed in "Troubleshooting" on page 149.

MARBLING PATTERNS

Freestyle Pattern

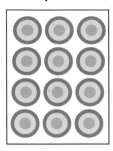

Apply drops of
different colors.

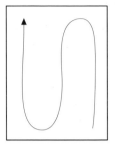

Pattern with stylus.

Spiral Pattern

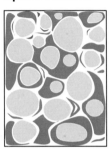

Apply drops of
different colors.

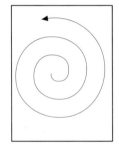

Pattern with stylus.

Waved Get-Gel Pattern

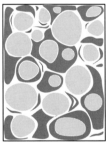

Apply drop of
different colors.

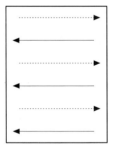

Pattern with 1" rake.

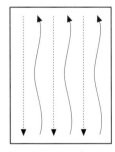

Pattern with 2" rake.

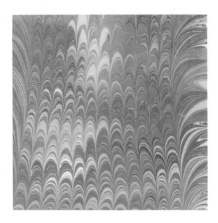

Nonpareil Pattern

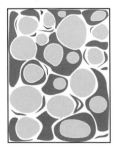

Apply drops of
different colors.

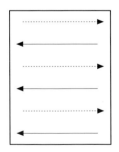

Pattern with 1" rake.

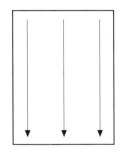

Pattern with ¼" comb.

TROUBLESHOOTING

The marbling colors sink into the size.

There are three possible causes: a skin may have formed on the size, the size may be too thick, and/or the marbling color(s) may need surfactant.

Try skimming the surface of the size with newspaper just before you apply drops of marbling color, adding water to the size and/or adding surfactant to the marbling color. Skim the size before each test drop and test between additions of surfactant. The more surfactant you add to the marbling color, the better it will float, the wider it will spread, and the lighter the color will be.

The marbling colors are spreading too fast.

There are two possible causes: the size may be too thin, and/or you may have added too much surfactant to the marbling colors.

To thicken the size, use 7 tablespoons (50 g) of methyl cellulose powder per gallon of water. If you think you have added too much surfactant, place drops of PRO Chem Colorless Extender on the surface of the size before testing marbling colors. The Extender changes the surface tension and slows the spread of the marbling colors.

The marbling colors floating on the size appear grainy.

The paint in the marbling color has settled. Shake the bottles of marbling color well before each use.

The drops of marbling color have jagged edges.

A skin has formed on the size. Skim the surface of the size and reapply the marbling colors.

The colors wash off the fabric in the rinse bucket and the remaining colors are pale, uneven, and streaked.

There are three possible causes: there may be a finish on the fabric, the alum soak may be too weak, and/or the alum soak may be too strong.

If you think you may not have adequately washed the fabric, scour it again (see pages 22–24). If the alum soak is too weak, it cannot hold the colors on the fabric. If the alum soak is too strong, the colors will adhere to the alum and will flake off in the rinse. If you think the solution is too weak or strong, make a new alum soak.

This fabric is a good candidate for shadow marbling.

There are white or dark fold marks in the marbled areas. 4

Either the fabric did not uniformly absorb the alum while it was in the soak or it was not laid down properly on the marbling colors. Soak smaller pieces of fabric and stir frequently. You may also need to practice laying the fabric down smoothly.

The fabric is fragile and rips after marbling.

Did you use a hot iron? Line dry the fabric after the alum soak. Use only a cool iron on fabric treated with alum. If the fabric was soaked in alum more than three weeks earlier, the alum may have caused the fabric to disintegrate.

There are white fractures in the marbled pattern. 5

There was a thread on the surface of the fabric. Trim all excess threads from the fabric before marbling.

> *Marbled Shirt*
by Robin Golinski for Robin Boston, 1994, Boston, Massachusetts. **Method**: Textile paints on cotton. Hand marbled.

Appendixes

Appendix A: Helpful Terms

Auxiliary products: The term for products used to assist the dye process. These products help the dye penetrate the fabric (for even color, lightfastness, and washfastness.

Cellulose: Fiber that is of plant origin, such as cotton, linen, ramie, flax, jute, or viscose rayon (regenerated cellulose). Although silk is classified as a protein (animal) rather than as a cellulose fiber, you can still dye it using the processes outlined in this book.

Cure: The process of permanently fixing dyes or paints to fabric.

Dye concentrate: A concentrated mixture of water and dye that is added to immersion dye baths.

Dye lot: Fabric dyed at the same time with the same color.

Dye paste: A mixture of urea, water softener, sodium alginate, dye powder, and water used for stamping and other direct-application techniques.

Dye site: Location on the fiber where the reaction takes place.

Dye-stock solution: A solution of water, dye, and urea that is used for tie dye and other direct-application techniques.

Fiber-reactive dyes: Manufactured dyes that reacts chemically with cellulose fibers. I recommend Procion MX fiber-reactive dyes because they are easy to use and provide brilliant colors. These dyes are considered nontoxic.

Fiber-reactive dyes can be permanently applied to protein (animal) fibers with additional auxiliary products.

Fixative: A chemical that permanently fixes MX Fiber-Reactive Dyes to fabric.

Gutta: A type of resist (the word "gutta" actually means resist). This is a liquid with the consistency of syrup. When applied to fabric, it creates a barrier that keeps the dye solution within defined areas. Gutta is available in both water- and solvent-based forms.

Hand: The way fabric feels to the touch. Some textile paints and liquid resists can change the hand of the fabric, making it stiffer.

Hue: A synonym for "color," hue is the pure state of a color.

Intensity: The purity, or saturation, of a color.

Level dyeing: Even dyeing, without spotting or irregular color.

Marbling colors: Although you can thin many water-based textile paints for marbling, I recommend that you purchase paints that have been prepared for marbling. Preparing marbling colors from paints can be a time-consuming process. Fabric-marbling kits are available from art and craft stores and through mail-order suppliers.

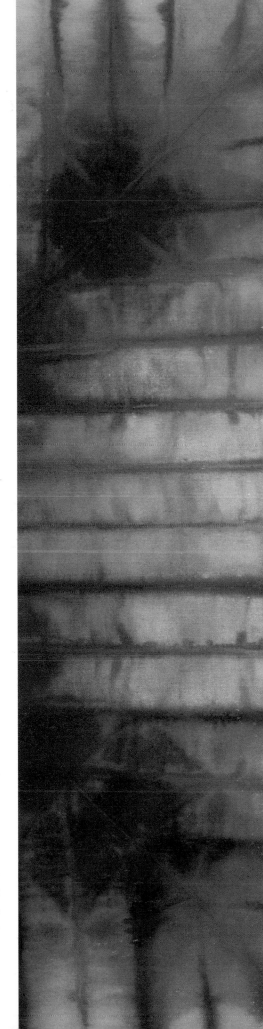

Marbling surfactant: This is the surface active agent that changes the surface tension of the marbling color. Marbling surfactant is added to the marbling colors to facilitate spreading or floating of the colors. Surfactants include Synthrapol, dish washing liquid, rubbing alcohol, and substances made specifically for marbling.

Each surfactant has a different capacity for altering the surface tension of the marbling color. Some, such as Synthrapol and rubbing alcohol, are very strong and should be used sparingly. For best results, I recommend marbling surfactants designed for marbling.

Maximum absorption point: The point of full saturation of a color. The maximum absorption point depends on the dye molecule's attainable depth of shade (which depends on its manufacturing) and the number of dye sites available on the fabric. Dye and fabric have independent maximum absorption points.

Mercerized cotton: Cotton is a single, elongated cell that, when dry, becomes flat and twists. The mercerization process produces microscopic changes in the appearance of the cell. The cotton is treated with caustic soda (sodium hydroxide) during the finishing process in manufacturing. The cotton cells swell and gradually untwist to produce a single tube—a fatter fiber. Because more light can reflect off the fatter fiber, the dyed, mercerized fabric appears, to our eyes, about 25% darker than unmercerized cotton treated with the same amount of dye. The mercerization treatment also improves the strength and increases the luster of the cotton fibers.

Overdye: To add color on top of a colored or patterned fabric.

Primary color: A color that cannot be made by mixing other colors: red, yellow, and blue.

Print paste: An inert mixture containing urea, water softener, sodium alginate (PRO Thick SH or F), and water. Print Paste controls the flow of the dye paste for direct-application dyeing techniques.

Procion: The trade name for the fiber-reactive dyes manufactured by BASF. The MX series is the most popular for home dyeing.

Reactivity rate: The rate at which dye molecules bond with fiber molecules. Some dyes, such as Procion Red MX-8B (Fuchsia 308) and Yellow MX-8G (Sun Yellow 108), react faster than others, which can effect the color of the dyed fabric.

Room temperature: The ideal temperature, 75° to 95° F (24° to 35° C), for MX Fiber-Reactive Dyes to permanently fix to fiber.

Scour: The first step in the dye process. This procedure removes excess wax, oil, dirt, and surface finishes.

Secondary color: A color that can be made by mixing two primary colors. Purple, orange, and green are secondary colors.

Shadow marbling: The process of marbling over another marbled design. (Marbled fabric must be treated again with alum before it can be shadow marbled.)

Shelf life: The length of time a product is useable. This can refer to the powdered state and/or the liquid state.

Size: Water that has been thickened so that marbling colors can float on top. There are many different thickeners used for marbling sizes, including methyl cellulose, carrageenan or Irish moss tea (seaweed), wallpaper paste, liquid starch, gelatin, and marbling medium.

I recommend methyl cellulose because it produces a smoother surface, is easier to prepare, has a longer shelf life, and is less expensive than other types of thickeners. Methyl cellulose is biodegradable and can be poured down the drain into any septic or disposal system.

Solubility level: The ability of a dye to dissolve. Low solubility means it will be more difficult to dissolve than a dye with high solubility. Some dyes, such as Yellow MX-8G (Sun Yellow 108), Red MX-8B (Fuchsia 308), and Blue MX-R (Basic Blue 400) dissolve slowly and take up more space in water. These dyes benefit from the addition of water or urea to the dye-stock solution or concentrate.

Substantivity: A dye's affinity for fiber. This relates to the ability of excess (unbonded) dye to rinse off fabric. Unbonded dye that is not properly removed in the final rinse and hot wash will come off in subsequent laundering, with the appearance of bleeding. Low substantivity means dye will wash off more easily than dye with high substantivity.

Textile paints: Insoluble organic or inorganic particles of color (pigment) that can be attached to fiber with a binder or adhesive.

Value: The lightness or darkness of a hue.

Appendix B: Helpful Products and Recipes

The following products are available at quilt shops, art and craft supply stores, and through mail-order suppliers.

Anti-chlor (sodium bisulfite): Chlorine is a strong oxidizing agent frequently used for stripping color in discharging processes. It has a strong affinity for fabric and does not completely wash out. An Anti-chlor bath is the safest way to remove traces of free chlorine, which, if left in fabric, will weaken it over time.

When using Anti-chlor, make sure there is ample ventilation, and wear safety goggles, a respirator, and gloves. Rinse each yard (91 cm) of fabric well in 95°F (35°C) water. While wearing a respirator and gloves, mix ¾ teaspoon (2 g) Anti-chlor in 1 gallon (4 L) of 110°F (44°C) water. Swish the fabric around for 15 minutes, then rinse well in room-temperature water. You can dry or redye the fabric without tenderizing it.

PROsoft: Fabric, in particular knits, can have a harsh hand or feel once they have been dyed. PROsoft is an industrial-strength liquid textile softener. It imparts a very soft hand without fragrances and is semipermanent. It can be applied in your washing machine and does not discolor fabric over time.

Wearing rubber gloves and safety goggles, mix 1 teaspoon (5 ml) per yard (91 cm) of fabric in 1 gallon (4 L) of 105° to 120°F (40° to 50°C) water. Swish the fabric around for 20 minutes or add PROsoft to the washing machine during the last rinse cycle. Do not rinse. Wring and dry fabric. Do not apply PROsoft if you plan to overdye your fabric; it will inhibit dye penetration.

Retayne: Retayne improves the colorfastness of *commercially* dyed fabrics that have a tendency to bleed when washed. It is especially useful for deep red and maroon shades. You can use Retayne in the washing machine or while hand washing.

Fill your washing machine with hot—140°F (60°C)—water. Heat water on the stove and add it to the machine if necessary. Add 1 teaspoon (5 ml) Retayne per yard (91 cm) of fabric. Add fabric and set the washing machine for a 20 minute wash. (Reset the washing machine, if necessary, so the Retayne does not go down the drain.) Rinse on warm cycle and dry at once. For subsequent laundering, wash the fabric in cool water.

Snowy Bleach (sodium perborate): If your fabric is not adequately rinsed and washed, the dye may bleed or "back stain"—leave a halo of color. Back staining is difficult to remove. Wash your fabric with Snowy Bleach (from the grocery store) according to the directions on the box. This frequently removes or lightens redeposited dye. If you notice staining while the fabric is wet, wash the fabric again in hot —140°F (60°C)—water with Synthrapol to remove excess dye.

Testing Commercial Fabric for Colorfastness

Dampen a 2" x 2" piece of white, 100% cotton muslin. Place this 2" square on the fabric to be tested. Iron the fabrics with a hot iron until dry. Inspect the muslin for color. If there has been some color transfer, treat the fabric with Retayne before washing.

Synthrapol: This is a surfactant (surface active agent) that interacts with the surface of the fiber, functioning as a lubricant. In essence, Synthrapol makes water wetter. Add Synthrapol to the dye bath to increase your fabric's absorbency, add a couple drops to dye concentrate to help dye powder dissolve, and use it to wash hand-dyed fabrics. Always wear gloves when using Synthrapol; it does a good job of cleaning the natural oils from your hands.

Appendix C: Weights of Auxiliary Products

The following weights were measured in a temperature- and humidity-controlled room and are approximate, because humidity affects weight. Some products compact when they are measured in large quantities. This accounts for the variations in weight between teaspoon, tablespoon, and cup measurements.

Product		Weight	
	Teaspoon	Tablespoon	Cup
Activator	3 g	9 g	153 g
Alum	4.4 g	14.4 g	
Anti-chlor	2.2 g	6.6 g	
Bicarbonate of soda	4.1 g	12 g	
Citric acid	5.8 g	17.5 g	
Metaphos	7 g	21 g	
Methyl cellulose	2.6 g	8 g	
Mixed alkali	3.1 g	10.8 g	
MX fiber-reactive dye	2.5g	9 g	
Print Paste Mix F	3.1 g	10.1 g	
Print Paste Mix SH	3.2 g	9.8 g	
PRO Chem Flakes (Ludigol)	2.3g	7.5g	
Salt, common table	5.6 g	14.8 g	299 g
Salt, glauber	6.6 g	20 g	
Thick F	3.2 g	9.9 g	
Thick SH	2.6 g	8.7 g	
Urea	4 g	12 g	

Appendix D: English and Metric Abbreviations, Measurements, and Conversion Charts

ENGLISH AND METRIC ABBREVIATIONS

" = inch

cm = centimeter

g = gram

gal = gallon

kg = kilogram

L = liter

lb = pound

m = meter

ml = milliliter

oz = ounce

qt = quart

Tbl = tablespoon

tsp = teaspoon

yd = yard

ENGLISH AND METRIC EQUIVALENCIES

Length

English

12 inches = 1 foot

3 feet = 1 yard

Metric

100 centimeters = 1 meter

English and Metric

1 inch = 2.54 centimeters

0.39 inch = 1 centimeter

39 inches = 1 meter

1 yard = 0.91 meter

Volume (Liquid Measure)

English

3 teaspoons = 1 tablespoon

16 tablespoons = 8 ounces (1 cup)

1 cup = 8 ounces

1 pint = 16 ounces (2 cups)

1 quart = 32 ounces (4 cups or 2 pints)

1 gallon = 128 ounces (16 cups or 4 quarts)

Metric

1 milliliter = 1 cubic centimeter

1,000 milliliters = 1 liter

English and Metric

1 teaspoon = 5 milliliters

1 tablespoon = 15 milliliters

1 ounce = 29.5 milliliters

1 cup = 236 milliliters (approximately 250 milliliters)

1 pint = 453 milliliters (approximately 500 milliliters)

1 quart = 946 milliliters (approximately 1 liter)

1 gallon = 3,784 milliliters (approximately 4 liters)

Weight (Dry Measure)

English

3 teaspoons = 1 tablespoon

2 tablespoons = 1 ounce

16 tablespoons = 1 cup (8 ounces)

2 cups = 1 pound (16 ounces)

Metric

1,000 grams = 1 kilogram

English and Metric

1 ounce = 28.5 grams

1 pound = 454 grams

2.2 pounds = 1 kilogram

English and Metric Conversion Charts

English to Metric Standards

To convert	into	multiply by
Lengths		
inches	mm	25.4
inches	cm	2.54
inches	meters	0.0254
feet	meters	0.3048
yards	meters	0.9144
Volumes		
cubic inches	cm³	16.387
cubic inches	liters	0.016387
cubic feet	m³	0.028317
cubic feet	liters	28.317
cubic yards	m³	0.7646
liquid ounces	cm³	29.57
gallons U.S.	m³	0.003785
gallons U.S.	liters	3.785
Weights		
ounces	grams	28.35
ounces	kg	0.02835
pounds	kg	0.4536

Metric to English Standards

To convert	into	multiply by
Lengths		
mm	inches	0.03937
cm	inches	0.3937
meters	inches	39.37
meters	feet	3.281
meters	yards	1.0936
Volumes		
cm³	liquid ounces	0.03381
m³	gallons U.S.	264.2
liters	gallons U.S.	0.2642
Weights		
grams	grains	15.432
grams	ounces	0.03527
kg	ounces	35.27
kg	pounds	2.2046

THERMOMETER COMPARISON

°F*	392	302	284	266	248	230	212	194	176	158	140	122	104	86	68	50	41	32
°C*	200	150	140	130	120	110	100	90	80	70	60	50	40	30	20	10	5	0

Here is a handy formula for converting Fahrenheit to Celsius (formerly Centigrade). Subtract 32 from the Fahrenheit temperature, then divide by 1.8. For example, 95°F - 32 = 63; 63 ÷ 1.8 = 35°C.

To change Celsius to Fahrenheit, multiply the Celsius figure by 1.8, then add 32. For example, 60°C x 1.8 = 108; 108 + 32 = 140°F.

Resources

United States

PRO Chemical & Dye
PO Box 14
Somerset, MA 02726
(508) 676-3838 (information)
1-800-2-BUY-DYE (phone orders) or
(508) 676-3980 (fax orders)
The products used in this book are distributed by PRO Chem. Free mail-order catalog includes a large selection of dyes, paints, tools and some fabrics. Instructions and customer support are available over the phone. On-site training facility with classes year 'round.

G&K Craft Industries, Ltd.
PO Box 38
Somerset, MA 02726-0038
Phone: 1-800-GKCRAFT
Wholesale for retail: dyes, paints, Presist

Alaska Dyeworks
300 W. Swanson, Suite 104
Wasilla, AK 99654
Phone: (907) 373-6562
Mail-order: Dyes and auxiliary products, dyed fabric

Dharma Trading Company
PO Box 150916
San Rafael, CA 94915
Phone: 1-800-542-5227
Mail-order and retail store: free catalog, dyes, paints, ready-to-dye garments

Lunn Fabrics
317 East Main Street
Lancaster, OH 43130
Phone: (614) 654-2202
Mail-order: PFD fabric

Qualin International
PO Box 31145
San Francisco, CA 94131
Phone: (415) 333-8500
Mail-order: Large selection of silk fabrics

Rupert, Gibbon and Spider, Inc.
PO Box 425
Healdsburg, CA 95448
Phone: 1-800-442-0455
Mail-order: free catalog, dyes, paints, fabrics

Testfabrics, Inc.
415 Delaware Avenue
PO Box 26
West Pittston, PA 18643
Phone: (717) 603-0432
Mail-order: free price list, large selection of PFD fabrics

Thai Silks
252 State Street
Los Altos, CA 94022
Phone: 1-800-722-7455 (or 1-800-221-SILK in California)
Mail-order: free price list, large selection of silk

Silkpaint Corporation
18220 Waldron Drive
PO Box 18-DP
Waldron, MO 64092
Phone: (816) 891-7774
Mail-order: Free price list; Silkpaint! Brand Water-Soluble Resist; the AirPen, for drawing lines on fabric with paint or resist

International Suppliers

Australia

Batik Oetoro Pty. Ltd.
203 Avoca Street
Randwick 2031
Phone: 02-9398-6201
Mail-order and retail store: dyes, paints, books, fabric

Canada

G&S Dye Accessories, Ltd.
250 Dundas Street West, Unit 8
Toronto, Ontario M5T 2Z5
Phone: 1-800-596-0550
Mail-order and retail store: dyes, paints, fabric

Maiwa Handprints, Ltd.
6-1666 Johnston Street
Vancouver, BC V6H 3S2
Phone: (604) 669-3939
Mail-order and retail store: dyes, paints

Denmark

Karen Noe Design
Søndergade 23
7171 Uldum
Phone: 45-7567-9733
Mail-order and retail store: dyes, paints, fabric

Germany

Galerie Smend
Mainzer Strasse 31
50678 Köln
Phone: 02-21/312047-48

United Kingdom

The Dyer's Hand
61 Hilton Road
Leeds LS8 4HA
Phone: (0113) 262-3791

George Weil & Sons Ltd.
The Warehouse
Reading Arch Road
Redhill, Surrey RH1 1HG
Phone: 0737-778868
Mail-order and retail store: dyes, paints, fabrics, books

Whaleys (Bradford) Ltd.
Harris Court, Great Horton
Bradford, West Yorkshire
BD7 4EQ
Phone: 01274-576718
Mail-order: PFD fabric

Bibliography

Albers, Josef. *Interaction of Color*. New Haven, Conn.: Yale University Press, 1975.

———. *An Outline of the Chemistry and Technology of the Dyestuffs Industry*. Manchester, England: ICI Colours & Fine Chemicals, 1968.

Blumenthal, Betsy and Kathryn Kreider. *Hands-on Dyeing*. Loveland, Colo.: Interweave Press, 1988.

Ingamells, Wilfred. *Colour for Textiles: A User's Handbook*. West Yorkshire, England: Society of Dyers and Colourists, 1993.

Johnson, Meda Parker and Glen Kaufman. *Design on Fabrics*. 2nd ed. New York: Van Nostrand Reinhold Company, 1981.

Klapper, Marvin. *Fabric Almanac*. New York: Fairchild Publications, Inc., 1966.

Maile, Anne. *Tie and Dye as a Present-Day Craft*. New York: Ballantine Books, 1963.

Nea, Sara. *Tie-dye: Designs, Materials, Technique*. New York: Van Nostrand Reinhold Company, 1971.

ICI Limited, Organics Division. *Procion Dyes: A Rational Basis of Dye Selection for Cotton, Pattern Leaflet 125*. Manchester, England, 1976.

Proctor, Richard and Jennifer Lew. *Surface Design for Fabric*. 2nd ed. Seattle: University of Washington Press, 1995.

Rivlin, Joseph. *The Dyeing of Textile Fibers, Theory and Practice*. Philadelphia: Philadelphia College of Textiles and Science, 1992.

Storey, Joyce. *The Thames and Hudson Manual of Dyes and Fabrics*. New York: Thames and Hudson, Inc., 1985.

Taylor, Carol. *Marbling Paper & Fabric*. New York: Sterling Publishing Co., Inc., 1991.

Trotman, E. R. *Dyeing and Chemical Technology of Textile Fibres*. London: Charles Griffin & Company Limited, 1975.

Wada, Rice, and Barton. *Shibori: The Inventive Art of Shaped Resist Dyeing*. Tokyo: Kodansha International, Ltd., 1983.

Wilcox, Michael. *Blue and Yellow Don't Make Green*. Cincinnati: Northlight Books, 1987.

Further Reading

BOOKS

Chambers, Anne. *Suminagashi: The Japanese Art of Marbling, A Practical Guide*. London: Thames and Hudson, Ltd., 1991.

Clark, Nancy, M.A.; Thomas Cutter, P.E.; Jean-Ann McGrane, M.S. *Ventilation: a Practical Guide for Artists, Craftspeople, and Others in the Arts*. New York: Center for Occupational Hazards, Inc., 1984.

Dunnewold, Jane. *Complex Cloth*. Bothell, Wash.: Fiber Studio Press, 1996.

Johnston, Ann. *Dye Painting!* Paducah, Ky.: American Quilter's Society, 1992.

Knutson, Linda. *Synthetic Dyes for Natural Fibers*. Seattle: Madrona Publishers, 1982.

Maurer, Diane Vogel and Paul Maurer. *Marbling: A Complete Guide to Creating Beautiful Patterned Papers and Fabrics*. New York: Friedman/Fairfax Publishers, 1994.

McCann, Michael, Ph.D., C.I.II. *Artist Beware*. New York: Lyons & Burford, 1992.

Moyer, Susan. *Silk Painting: The Artist's Guide to Gutta and Wax Resist Techniques*. New York: Watson-Guptill Publications, 1991.

Murashima, Kumiko. *Katazome: Japanese Paste-Resist Dyeing for Contemporary Use*. Asheville, N.C.: Lark Books, 1993.

Porcella, Yvonne. *Colors Changing Hue*. Lafayette, Calif.: C&T Publishing, 1994.

Rossol, Monona. *The Artist's Complete Health and Safety Guide*. New York: Allworth Press, 1990.

Laury, Jean Ray. *Imagery on Fabric*. Lafayette, Calif.: C&T Publishing, 1992.

Schleicher, Patty and Mimi Schleicher. *Marbled Designs: A Complete Guide to Fifty-Five Elegant Patterns*. Asheville, N.C.: Lark Books, 1993.

Wiener, Donald. *The Best of Q&A*. Surface Design Association, 1991.

Widger, Katy. *Color Wheel Fabric Dyeing*. Edgewood, N. Mex.: self-published, 1991.

Wolfrom, Joen. *The Magical Effects of Color*. Lafayette, Calif.: C&T Publishing, 1992.

Index

Biography

To affect the quality
of the day, that is the
highest of arts.

Henry David Thoreau

Describing herself as "fascinated and intrigued by the link between observation and visual design," Elin Noble is a fiber artist whose talents include papermaking, bookbinding, and dyeing cloth. She began working with dyes in the summer of 1977 while attending the University of Washington. Elin's work has been exhibited nationwide, and she has taught papermaking and dyeing classes throughout North America.

Elin lives and dyes in East Freetown, Massachusetts, with her husband and two dogs.